African American Church Management Handbook

Floyd H. Flake,
Elaine McCollins Flake,
and Edwin C. Reed

JUDSON PRESS
PUBLISHERS SINCE 1824

Valley Forge, PA

African American Church Management Handbook

© 2005 by Judson Press, Valley Forge, PA 19482-0851
All rights reserved.

Judson Press has made every effort to trace the ownership of all quotes. In the event of a question arising from the use of a quote, we regret any error made and will be pleased to make the necessary correction in future printings and editions of this book.

Bible quotations in this volume are from the *The Holy Bible*, King James Version. (KJV)

Library of Congress Cataloging-in-Publication Data

Flake, Floyd.
African American church management handbook / Floyd H. Flake, Elaine McCollins Flake, Edwin C. Reed.
p. cm.
ISBN 0-8170-1485-3 (alk. paper)
1. African American churches. 2. Church management—United States. I. Flake, Elaine McCollins. II. Reed, Edwin C. III. Title.
BR563.N4F53 2005
254'.0089'96073—dc22   2005023390

Printed in the U.S.A.

13 12 11 10 09 08 07 06 05   10 9 8 7 6 5 4 3 2 1

African American Church Management Handbook

ASCPL DISCARDED

We dedicate this book with gratitude
to the members of The Greater Allen A.M.E. Cathedral
for their commitment to the vision of
efficient financial management
and expansive community development;
who along with our many partners
made it possible to bring our ideas to fruition.

Contents

Preface

MANY A PASTOR, UPON TAKING HIS OR HER FIRST CHURCH, IS surprised to discover that the job description and expectations of the pastor differ from what he or she had thought. Most pastors, in accepting a call from the Lord, had in mind that they were called to preach the Word, not to run a business.

Indeed, especially in the African American church, the pastor finds a great sense of joy and fulfillment in stepping into the pulpit—providing words of comfort and hope, and words of challenge, to individuals, as well as prophetic messages to the powerbrokers of society. Many of these same preachers are considerably less excited about creating a budget, managing a staff, and attending a seemingly endless array of meetings. As a result, African American pastors by and large are better preachers than they are administrators.

What's more, seminaries in general have not done enough to prepare pastors for the day-to-day tasks associated with managing a church, which, as we will see, in many ways resembles a business and ought to be regarded as such. The church administration component of a parish is no different from that of any business or corporation.

This book is designed to help pastors balance the challenging roles that are attendant to the call to "preach." Effective church management is directly related to successful church ministry. Preaching is perhaps most important, but ministry is not all about preaching. Some reputations are built on the ability of the pastor to properly manage the affairs and business of the church. Effective ministry also requires such things as properly managing staff, thorough evaluation of ministry effectiveness, and efficient and faithful stewardship of God's resources, including the church's financial resources. The best of all worlds is when the pastor can do most things well and delegate in areas where he or she has weaknesses.

Ultimately, the seemingly mundane aspects of ministry cannot be separated from those aspects deemed more "spiritual." After all, the pastor's ability to proclaim the Word and to lead God's people with integrity can be severely damaged if there are questions about misuse of the church's money or improprieties related to staff persons. The reality is that *everything* a church does or does not do has some influence on its effectiveness in ministry; thus the need for a contemporary resource on church management in the African American context.

Much more could be said about virtually all the topics we have addressed in this book. Our goal is to provide helpful perspectives and practical advice on a wide range of topics—from the pastor's management style to running a business meeting to creating a budget to forming a nonprofit corporation. The Table of Contents provides a more complete list of topics covered.

We have based much of our information and perspectives on our experience at The Greater Allen A.M.E. Cathedral in Jamaica Queens, New York. It is a church that many have found to be a worthy model of successful church management, as well as effective community and economic development. However, we pray that in your reading of the book you will not be intimidated by our examples. Allen started small and grew to become a mega-church. This book will hopefully help you realize that God has given you new tools to grow the church and enhance the kingdom.

We wish to acknowledge our families, the many members of The Greater Allen A.M.E. Cathedral, and the South East Queens and New York communities for their love and support. Furthermore, we acknowledge the editorial work of Randy Frame and the Judson Press staff, as well as Christina London, whose dedication to the project was immeasurable.

About Greater Allen A.M.E.

THE ALLEN AFRICAN METHODIST EPISCOPAL CHURCH, NOW known as The Greater Allen African Methodist Episcopal Cathedral of New York and located on Merrick Boulevard in Jamaica Queens, New York, was founded in 1834. Dr. Floyd H. Flake has served as pastor since 1976. In 1998, his spouse, Elaine Flake, was named copastor.

The church has grown from 1,200 members in 1976 to more than 20,000 members today with an asset base of $106 million. Its more than 300 employees make Greater Allen A.M.E. and its subsidiaries one of the largest employers in the borough of Queens.

The church's varied and far-reaching ministries include the following: Women's Ministry; Men's Ministry; Shekinah Youth Ministry; Sunday School; Young Adult Ministry; Outreach Ministry, which addresses the physical needs of the community; Membership Nurture, which cares for the sick, shut-ins, and those in mourning; Elizabeth Support Group, which raises funds to enrich the educational, cultural, and spiritual development of students at the Allen Christian School; Counseling Ministry; Discipleship Ministry; Worship and Arts Ministry;

Allen Christian Theatre; Allen Liturgical Dance Ministry; Creative Arts Ministry; Communications/Media Ministry; Music Ministry; Security Ministry; Sign Language Ministry; Step Ministry; the Usher Ministry; and many more, totaling more than 120 categories of service.

The church operates 630 senior citizen housing units and 15 veterans' apartments, as well as 54 residential housing units and 9 commercial stores. Among its subsidiary organizations are the following:

■ Allen/Reliance Federal Credit Union, serving church members and related corporations

■ Allen Christian School, which serves 650 students in grades pre-K through eight

■ Allen Transportation, a full service, for-profit bus transportation and charter business

■ Allen Women's Resource Center, a safe haven for women and children who have been victimized by domestic violence

■ South Jamaica Multi-Service Center, which provides various social services to the community, including medical care, a G.E.D. program, Head Start programs, and support services for those transitioning from homelessness to home ownership

■ Allen Senior Citizens Community Center, which provides nutritional, medical, and other services to the elderly

■ Allen Consortium for Community Empowerment Stabilization & Service, which assists people in transition from welfare to work

■ Allen Housing Development Fund, a federally funded senior citizen apartment complex

■ Allen A.M.E. Housing, which rehabilitates homes and owns and operates commercial stores and rental apartments

■ Allen Veteran Housing Corporation, which helps veterans to live independently

■ Allen Christian Bible Institute, which offers a wide range of courses in theology, Bible (Old and New Testament), and homiletics.

In addition, Nyack College offers continuing education courses at Allen leading to college degrees for adults who have completed 60 or more credits.

1

Distinctive Characteristics of African American Churches

NOTE: Unless otherwise noted, the first person "I" refers to Rev. Floyd H. Flake.

WHEN RICHARD ALLEN, ABSALOM JONES, AND OTHERS GAVE birth to the first black churches in the United States, the focus was on empowerment. This is evident in part from the songs these churches sang, liberation songs that envisioned a better future in heaven after a life of struggle on earth.

Individuals gained a sense of empowerment in the church. There a person who was a servant during the week acted as trustee, deacon, or steward. Historically the church has been a place where African American people, especially men, have found the self-esteem they have been denied in the larger culture.

Much has changed over the years. Today's African American pastors are far more likely to be educated than in the past; many have master's degrees, and a significant number have earned doctorates. Unlike in previous years, many are marketable in other careers. They are not in ministry by default; rather, they pastor out of a sense of calling. This sense of calling—as opposed to a career choice—is more pronounced in the African American context than it is in the white church culture.

History's Influences

Although much has changed, many of the influences of our history remain. Ours is a church born out of slavery in this country. As the black population moved from plantations in the South to work at steel mills and automobile plants in the North, it continued to face injustice and discrimination. And in the absence of political leaders, African Americans continued to look to the church for hope and guidance. The church became not only the voice of God to the people of God who were oppressed, but also to the conscience of the oppressor. From the churches came the NAACP, schools for blacks, burial associations, and various social organizations.

Because African American people by and large still have a unique sense of connection to church and to God, they make decisions based primarily on what they believe God requires. And their understanding of what God requires is shaped in large part by what they hear on Sunday mornings in God's message from the preacher.

Black pastors today, as in the past, are regarded with a level of esteem that exceeds that of almost any other person in leadership. The wives of many black pastors are known as "first ladies," and as more and more first ladies accept the call to preach, they become copastors. In public settings, black parishioners, upon introducing themselves, as a matter of course proclaim with pride the name of their church and their pastor.

Yet another of history's legacies has to do with power. Traditionally the African American community's ability to influence the larger society has been limited. Thus, those who have found some measure of influence in the church have tended to try to hold on to this power or gain more of it. This dynamic has produced various conflicts and territorial squabbles in the African American church context.

Journey to Freedom

Though the specific issues have changed, most African American preachers continue to view their mission in terms of bringing oppressed people to freedom—from Egypt to the Promised Land, from slavery to freedom. In fact, the journey from the plantation to full freedom is one that few black pastors would dare to believe has been completed.

In general, the priority issues of black churches differ from the issues that are of importance in the white church context. The African American church has focused on issues related to civil rights, poverty, and justice. Organizations representing the so-called Christian Right (which is predominately white) have focused largely on issues such as abortion, gay marriage, and prayer in schools.

Many white pastors don't understand why the black church does not speak out more forcefully on "their" issues, many of which are related to personal holiness and righteousness. They do not realize that in the black church an inordinate number of boys are in jail, too many girls are producing babies out of wedlock, and too many children are not getting a proper education in the school system. Issues of ethics, righteousness, and personal holiness are important to black pastors, and they do preach about them, but these issues do not overshadow the issues that affect people who still, to varying degrees, are experiencing oppression or its aftereffects.

A Contemporary Prophetic Message

Up through the civil rights era, Martin Luther King Jr. and other leaders of the black community were primarily preachers. These preachers spoke the language of a prophetic gospel modeled after the Old Testament prophets.

While it is important to acknowledge with profound respect the contributions of previous generations of preachers, it is essential that contemporary preachers move to a different place. We need to redefine to some extent past models of preaching and leadership. The reality is that much of what we as a people have fought for we have gained. Yet, despite the availability of financial aid, too few African American people are going to school. And although the Voting Rights Act was passed in 1965, too few are going to the polls. And despite the passage of fair housing laws, a hugely disproportionate percentage of African American people own homes.

Thus, while all preachers—black and white—must continue to speak prophetically to the powers that be, we must also speak prophetically to that which is *within* the person. We must challenge people to take responsibility, to move beyond expecting things to come by external means, and to focus on their own role in the process.

2

The Ministry of the Church

THE CHURCH CONSISTS OF THOSE WHO HAVE ACCEPTED JESUS Christ as their Savior and who have dedicated their lives as disciples to following Jesus' teachings and example. The church's mission, stated generally, is to serve as God's witnesses or ambassadors to people who are in need.

The needs of the people range from the spiritual to the psychological and emotional to the physical and economic. The borders between and among these various realms overlap. Thus, ideally the church ought to take a holistic approach to caring for others, an approach that emphasizes helping people draw nearer to God (Acts 2:41-47).

All persons are created in the image of God, and it is the role of the church to help people identify and lay claim to the essential goodness that lies within them. We accomplish this by bringing people into a relationship with God through Christ, who is the source of all goodness, and by facilitating the growth of this relationship. This is the essence of evangelism.

In contemplating evangelistic ministry, the pastor and church leadership ought to recognize that not all who attend church—even those who attend regularly—are saved. Therefore the church's evangelistic ministry must in some way touch the people within the church as well as those who are outside of it. At least on occasion, people who attend church ought to be given the opportunity to enter into a relationship with Christ without feeling any sense of shame or embarrassment.

Among the keys to successful evangelism is setting a good example. Hence it is especially important for the pastor and other church leaders to live with integrity. If a picture is worth a thousand words, an example is worth ten thousand. People will be drawn to the church as a result of a good example, but will be repelled if the leadership represents a bad example of the teachings of Christ.

Making Disciples

The chief calling of the church is not to make new members, but to make *disciples*. Indeed, it is crucial for the church to make disciples, for disciples make other disciples. Thus, a person's joining the church should mark the beginning, not the end, of a process. Such persons should be a part of a new members class (at Greater Allen, it lasts for eight weeks) in which they learn more about the Christian faith, the denomination and/or Christian heritage of which the church is a part, and the mission and ministries of the church.

This class should be followed up by discipleship classes (at Allen, the classes last for twelve weeks) so that these new Christians can continue to grow in their faith and learn more about opportunities to get involved in the ministries of the church and can establish a foundation to support their beliefs.

Because the Bible is the source of spiritual wisdom and

growth in faith, all new members (and older ones for that matter) should have access to various opportunities for group Bible study, whether as part of a men's, women's, youth, or young adult fellowship or in a study led by one of the pastors.

Worship

Meaningful, moving, challenging, life-changing worship is essential to the life and growth of the church. Sunday worship is the weekly opportunity for the local body of Christ to gather to praise God, to be fed by the Word of God, and to enjoy fellowship with one another. If visitors come to a dead place, they are not likely to return. The service should be lively, and no time should be wasted on superfluous, nonessential matters.

The African American church traditionally has been characterized by an emphasis on the spontaneous moving of the Holy Spirit. This explains in part why the sermon and the service are not so bound by time as they are in other Christian worship traditions. Overall, this is a very healthy dynamic in that it emphasizes *experiencing* God and not just learning about God.

However, decency and order must be the rule. We must be careful not to allow emphasis on the moving of the Spirit to serve as an excuse for a lack of preparation or order. There has to be some structure even as the church grants leeway to movement of the Holy Spirit. In the past, people came to church no matter the nature of the service. But today, if the worship service appears to be in disarray, people won't come consistently.

As will be explored more fully later, the church, in addition to being a ministry, is a business. It may be the only business in which the CEO (i.e., the pastor) has an opportunity each week to address in person all of his or her "colaborers" and supporters. Effective pastors make the most of this opportunity not only in the sermon, but also in the pastoral remarks and in the design of the worship service. This entails putting some thought into what message(s) the church leadership wants to introduce or highlight in any given week.

There is no one right way to structure the worship service, but the structure should be consistent from week to week. Familiarity breeds comfort. At Allen we begin with prayer and twenty minutes of praise and worship. Then we have an offering to support missionary and educational work, followed by announcements. Next we pray for the sick and those who have other prayer concerns. Then we recognize visitors, take the main offering, and read the Scripture, which is followed by the sermon. After the sermon the structure is more fluid because we cannot predict how the Spirit will move or how many will come to the altar to receive Christ as their personal Savior.

The Sermon

In the African American church, the integrity of the worship service centers on the sermon. Thus, developing a quality message each week must be high on the pastor's list of priorities. The best sermons are those that go beyond giving people the feeling of emotional catharsis, important though that is. A sermon should challenge and empower people to do something about their lives: to fix a troubled marriage, to go back to college, to save money to buy a home, to get more involved in one of the church's ministries.

At Allen we have three Sunday morning services each week (6:30, 8:30, and 11:15), of which I preach at two. (On most Sundays, Rev. Elaine preaches at one of the services.) I write and preach two new sermons each week because I'm not comfortable preaching the same sermon twice in the same setting. I write these sermons by Thursday so I can live with them until the preaching moment in Sunday service.

With regard to music and worship style, because the world is constantly changing, the church should be careful not to limit itself or get stuck in old patterns. Tommy Dorsey, James Cleveland, Walter Hawkins, and Shirley Caesar prove that there is nothing wrong with rearranging a hymn to give it a contemporary sound. We need to embody these changes in our music forms and in the lyrics. At Allen we are very aware of the fact that our largest growth in population is in the 18–35 age range.

Churches should not underestimate the importance of good music. If at all possible, a church should hire professional musicians who are committed believers and who are also committed to the highest quality of music ministry.

Finally, the elements of the worship service ought to be coordinated. Any special music or anthems, for example, should support the pastor's message for that day. Those participating in the worship service should hold regular meetings for the purpose of planning worship in ways that contribute to a unified theme or message.

Outreach

The apostle Peter had to find a way to meet the needs of grieving widows. He recruited Stephen. Likewise, in its outreach efforts, a church should be alert and sensitive to the needs of the people and then form ministries to address them. A church should do its best to provide a ministry to address every need within the congregation and the community. The range of needs for ministry offers great opportunities. If a bereavement ministry is needed, the church should have one. If senior citizens need care, the church should meet their needs.

Education ranks among the most critical areas of ministry. We ought to do more than just preach about the problems associated with the educational system. Too many of our children are getting lost and dying in the system. When this happens, these children disappear from the church and become part of the prison population.

If a church determines to assess and meet the needs of its community, it almost cannot help but grow. If a church starts a school or tutoring program for children, some of those children will bring their parents to church. If a church starts programs for senior citizens, some of those seniors' sons and daughters will come to church.

The point here is that people (and in many cases their families and friends) come to the place where they are being served. Many churches focus on Sunday morning attendance. But you will not have to worry about people coming on Sunday morning if you are meeting their needs the other six days of the week.

All churches are sometimes asked to host weddings or funeral services. At Allen we charge a fee for weddings, since we regard this as a choice people make. But people do not choose to die. Thus, we consider administering funeral services part of our ministry to the community. We have two ministers on staff whose responsibilities are focused on ministry to the bereaved. Churches must go beyond being content being *in* community to seeing themselves as being part *of* the community. This approach has contributed significantly to Allen's growth as a church. Again, people who are served by the church will be drawn to the church. One of the important ways to serve people is to minister to family members when they have lost a loved one.

We learn from the book of Acts that the early church was adding to its numbers daily. A church cannot add to its numbers daily if it is closed daily. In this regard, the church, as we will explore more fully later, must think of itself not only as a ministry, but as a business. Good stewardship demands it. Churches are the only business I know that make a major investment in a capital asset—namely, a building—and then allow it to operate only one day a week, except perhaps for a mid-week Bible study or choir rehearsal. This is a poor investment. A church ought to be open and functioning daily.

A local church, because of limitations of human and financial resources, cannot do all the things it would like to do as quickly as it might like to do them. Therefore it is important for the church to determine sensible ministry priorities. Too many churches fail to accurately assess their environment, and thus they spend time, effort, and money "majoring in the minors" instead of providing what the people need most.

Churches that desire to do more ministry must commit to growth spiritually, numerically, and economically. The three are, of course, related. Churches must move beyond any shyness they have about acknowledging that it takes financial resources to hire professionally trained staff and to plan and carry out ministry activities that accomplish the church's mission.

Openness to Change

Many churches don't grow because they won't change, even though the world is constantly changing around them. Some people say they would be willing to do anything to get their children or grandchildren to come to church—anything, that is, except change the worship service to make it more contemporary and relevant. The insistence on putting "new wine in old skins" has killed the potential of many churches to attract young people.

God is not a God of stagnation! If a local church is not

growing, it needs to ask itself why. It needs to find out why members stay at home or visit other churches and why young people are not coming. Then it must make appropriate changes to address the problem. It might help churches to observe what growing churches in their area are doing to attract new people. But this is wasted effort if the church is not open to making changes.

Hesitance to change affects the church's ability to keep new members. It is possible to make people feel at home in their new church for a few weeks, but integrating them into the life of the church is another issue, especially if current members are concerned that the newcomers might impinge on their leadership territory or upset the social relationships with which they are familiar and have become comfortable. Ironically, sometimes new people and new ideas are exactly what a church needs to get out of the rut it is in. (See also "Managing Change," p. 60.)

Incorporating New Members

Many churches do a wonderful job of welcoming new members but a poor job of incorporating them into the life of the church. New member classes are a crucial step in accomplishing this goal. Churches should also hold receptions for new members upon the completion of the class. Such an event is an ideal occasion for the ministries of the church to set up tables or distribute brochures describing various opportunities for newcomers—based on their needs, gifts, and interests—to plug into the life of the church. As noted above, all new members should be encouraged to become a part of a regular Bible study.

No matter what the church does programmatically, however, it will have trouble drawing and incorporating new people if it lacks an overall spirit of friendliness. This spirit must include, especially among the church's leaders, a conscious effort to care about newcomers and to make sure they are making connections and feeling at home in the church.

Making people feel welcome and loved within the church environment is a commitment that ought to begin in the pulpit and extend all the way to the back door. Pastors should make other people feel good about being around them. You cannot behave in ways that send the message that you are too high and mighty to speak to God's people. In addition to being their preacher, counselor, teacher, and guide, the pastor must be a friend (within prescribed limits, as will be addressed later) to the people. This kind of spirit can be communicated in simple ways, for example, by making the rounds among various offices and classrooms, popping in and saying, "Hello. It's good to see you here." This communicates to people that, no matter how busy the pastor may be, he or she is accessible.

The Church as a Business

The local church should never lose sight of its identity as a ministry. As suggested earlier, this entails a strong, uncompromising commitment to integrity in its preaching and teaching, as well as an understanding of its role as a change agent for the larger community.

On the other hand, the church must recognize that it is also a business. Indeed, there is a sense in which the church *ought* to operate as a business, given the need to generate revenue to meet operational and ministry needs. Of course, the church should not be all about money. If that is the case, it ceases to be a ministry. But neither can it ignore financial realities. A church needs to bring in resources not just to function, but to be successful in maximizing its capability as a ministry.

Ultimately, the ministry and business aspects of the church's identity cannot be separated. After all, the business of the church *is* ministry. The church is in the business of saving souls, helping people move from a life of sin to salvation and from where they are to where they ought to be in terms of their relationship with God. To put it another way, the business objective of the church (which is also the ministry objective) is to help people grow in spirit, ethics, values, virtues, purpose, and pursuit of the more excellent way.

Although money is not the primary objective, meeting the business objective (saving souls) has financial implications that church leaders ought not to deny or suppress. The business of the church is to bring souls into the kingdom, and the souls that are blessed by the church generate tithes and offerings that support additional ministry.

Some may feel uncomfortable talking about the church's ministry in this way. But this is the reality, for which there is considerable biblical support. Church leaders ought never to think of people strictly in terms of their income-generating potential, but neither should they consider it taboo to discuss the relationship between adding people to the church and generating revenue for the church's ministries. Churches that are hesitant to discuss financial realities are more likely to operate on a "hand-to-mouth" basis, struggling each month to pay bills. This approach casts a dim light on the church.

In contrast, churches that are up-front in addressing financial realities are more likely to dream about and consider new ministry possibilities, rather than worry about how to pay the mortgage, utilities, insurance, and other bills. People don't come to church to hear that it is struggling with the same issues they are confronting at home.

This said, however, one of the biggest dangers to the church is to have leaders who may be good businesspeople but don't fully understand or appreciate that the business of the church is first and foremost Christian ministry. This opens the door to the possibility of forgetting that the hearts and spirits of people need to remain highest on the church's list of priorities.

A church that models a healthy integration of business and ministry uplifts the kingdom in everything it does, whether planning the worship service, preparing a financial report, or adding a building to assist the growth of ministry. Ultimately everything we do ought to point back to God's goodness.

MARKET ANALYSIS No business would ever operate in an area without understanding its market. For a church, this principle translates into knowing the key demographic facts about church members and the surrounding community. Is it an aging population or a young one? What is the racial composition? What do people do for a living? What do they do with their spare time? What are their perceived needs? The answers to these and other questions will guide the creation and shaping of church ministries. (See also "Assessing the Environment," p. 24.)

At Allen we track membership weekly. Our report indicates deaths, new members (by their ages and gender), and financial contributions.

MANAGING RESOURCES Ministries or businesses that operate effectively make use of all the resources available to them. (See also chapter 7, "Managing Money.") They manage these resources, including human resources, efficiently and with care and compassion. When individuals in the church are expected to do more than they are capable of doing—or are doing things they are not qualified or gifted to do—the ministry of the church suffers.

Unfortunately, in many churches, especially small churches, the pastor is expected to do everything, which means that he or she is not able to fully exercise his or her gifts. Pastors can address this problem initially by building systems with volunteers. As the church grows, based on its needs and priorities, the church can replace these volunteers with professional staff.

The Church Staff

At minimum a church ought to have three paid or pro bono employees (even if they are only part-time): a pastor, a sexton (maintenance person), and a secretary. Having someone to look after the physical facility and to handle routine office work, such as answering phones and typing the church bulletin, goes a long way toward freeing the pastor to concentrate on developing ministry and preparing sermons or Bible studies.

From here a church can begin to grow and develop. Churches typically have a ministry vision that is greater than the staff is able to carry out. Thus, it becomes a priority to identify and employ the skills and talents of volunteers. The important roles volunteers can play in the ministry of a church ought never be dismissed or diminished. However, growing a progressive, more professional, and farther-reaching ministry will require at some point the addition of professional staff. No matter how faithful volunteers might be, they are generally people who have full-time responsibilities or jobs and serve the church on the side. Professional staff are able to contribute more consistently, not only because of their training, but because, as with anyone, their vocation is high on their list of priorities. Paid staff can also be held accountable to higher standards than volunteers.

Where to begin adding professional staff will differ according to a church's specific needs and ministry vision. The first addition might be an assistant pastor, or a minister of music, a youth pastor, or a Christian education director.

Churches typically consider whether they can afford to hire another staff person. But when a church reaches a certain level and aspires to continue to grow, it must also conduct a needs assessment to determine whether it can afford *not* to hire new staff. For example, if a church begins to receive government funding or is working with financial institutions to secure loans, expectations of quality in financial statements increase markedly. A chief financial officer who understands finance will be of greater value than a bookkeeper who may be an excellent keeper of financial records but whose qualifications do not meet the standards of the funding entity.

There is almost always a correlation between a growing church and increased financial resources. Thus, adding staff persons should result in additional ministry and in growth, including financial growth. Churches should plan for continued growth, which justifies the hiring of additional staff.

Church Officers

Those who are elected or appointed to serve as church officers ought to be among the church's most respected spiritual leaders. All elders, deacons, stewards, trustees, ushers, and others in leadership ought to be people who have a mature relationship with God. Certainly they must be tithers. It doesn't make sense to put people in charge of other people's money if they have not demonstrated responsibility with their own.

The specific roles or functions of church officers may vary from church to church. In general, elders, deacons, and stewards are responsible for the spiritual life of the church. This can unfold in many different ways, but these persons are basically extensions of the pastor, thus the importance of their commitment to leading ethical and disciplined lives.

Trustees are primarily responsible for finances of the church and its general operation. The trustees are, in essence, the board of the corporation. They too must meet the requirement of leading ethical and disciplined lives.

Ushers are the doorkeepers of the house of the Lord. Their responsibilities include recognizing new people and making them feel welcome in the church.

At Allen, although the officers have primary responsibilities, we try not to define their roles too narrowly. For example, the stewards and the trustees all take turns counting the money, visiting the sick, and participating in worship. Thus they are fully engaged in the life of the church, as opposed to being confined to a single area. If all they do is count money, they have a tendency to fall in love with that responsibility and ignore the others.

Unfortunately, in some churches various officers and church boards end up in tension with one another. Perhaps there is some competition or disagreement over who should be doing what, especially with regard to controlling the money. This is partly why at Allen we hold a joint meeting of all stewards and trustees once a month. This helps us to iron out any contentious issues and to realize that we all are ultimately working toward accomplishing the same goals for the good of God's ministry. By having officers in a collective meeting, there is no room for either group to feel that it has jurisdiction or proprietary rights over the others.

Structure

Exercising the best stewardship over the resources that come into the church requires an efficient, effective structure, one that supports and enhances the church's ministry goals and objectives. There is no place or time for battles over control of what belongs to God.

Perhaps the single most relevant model from the business world that the church ought to apply is the model that calls for autonomous entities operating within the larger organization. For example, the marriage enrichment, youth, young adult, and missionary ministries each have goals that are best pursued with autonomy, but consistent with the church's vision.

The most significant step in operating autonomously is for each ministry entity to develop its own mission statement and programs. In the African American context, many longstanding groups, such as the "Willing Workers," have lost a vital ministry edge. Many of them were founded with a focus on fundraising instead of on service. They resist reinvention or redefinition. Redefining ministry goals can give such organizations a whole new sense of purpose and vitality. And putting these goals in writing serves to keep the ministry accountable.

The Pastor as Manager

Pastors must recognize that they have two very distinct roles in the church. The first is to serve as the spiritual shepherd, prophet, priest, and preacher of the people. The pastor's second role is that of manager. In essence, the pastor is the organization's CEO. (See also chapter 6, "Managing People.")

Although these two roles are distinct, they must be considered together. The pastor cannot be one personality on Sunday morning and a different personality during the week. If that is the case, the inevitable result will be conflict and tension both for the pastor and the congregation. The pastor's management style ought to be consistent with the values and attitudes he or she communicates in worship. These values should permeate the pastor's role as manager throughout the week. In this role the pastor ought to be supportive but not needing to control everything; he or she should be directive but not autocratic.

In addition, the pastor must recognize his or her limitations when it comes to managing the church. Most people who enter the pastoral ministry do not have a business background or orientation. Seminary does not train pastors to run businesses. Even the church administration classes typically offered at seminary do not focus on the pastor's role as CEO.

Thus, a pastor is wise to identify his or her areas of weakness in financial management and/or administration and take steps to plug any gaps. This entails finding the right people to serve the church either as paid staff or on a volunteer basis. Such persons, of course, should exhibit strong business acumen. Again, however, it is especially important for them to recognize that the business of the church is ministry. Unfortunately, some may think they are in a superior position to the pastor because they manage the money.

Jesus' admonition that the love of money is the root of all evil certainly applies to the one who controls the purse strings. Such persons can make or break ministry. If they are zealous about their role and place with God, they will likely do much to enhance the church's ministry. But if they revel in having control, they will stifle the ministry, cause its potential to wilt, or at least prevent it from achieving its maximum potential. In some cases, achieving maximum potential requires changing personnel.

3

Vision for Ministry

A CHURCH'S VISION OUGHT TO BEGIN WITH THE RECOGNITION that God gives supernatural revelations for the church through the imaginative contemplation of its leadership. Within the context of this reality, the church's role is to determine how its ministry fits into God's vision so that opportunities can be fulfilled in the lives of God's people.

Vision and Flexibility

A vision for ministry does not have to be understood in terms of waking up in the middle of the night because God has laid "this thing" on you. A vision can be developed largely as a result of the challenges presented by the church's immediate environment in concert with an assessment of available resources. For example, a church is located in a community wherein a high percentage of residents are elderly, especially if these people are unchurched, ought to consider, based on the need, starting programs (perhaps a daytime Bible Study) for seniors.

In the late 1970s, the community surrounding Greater Allen Cathedral was considered to be a middle class community in decline. Whereas it had once been an upscale community, including black people of some means and standing, it was suffering from both white flight and black flight to the suburbs. Housing and social services were in decline, as was the educational system. But the one thing the community had plenty of was vacant land. Most of it belonged to the city and had been earmarked for urban renewal. The church reached out to the city and the federal government to determine what could be done with the empty land and the deteriorating houses.

Having come out of higher education, where I witnessed the shortcomings of so many minority students from urban communities, my vision was to build a school. But the government program available at the time focused on senior citizen housing. We communicated with the Department of Housing and Urban Development and wound up building what was, at the time, the largest senior citizen complex in the country under the Section 202 program of the Older Americans Act of 1976. We had no idea that this effort would serve as a sort of launching pad for larger scale community economic development and restoration of the community.

I didn't let go of the original vision. In fact, the more I saw what was happening to our children in public education, the more I clung to the vision of creating a model school for children pre-K through eighth grade to help them to become as college-ready as most kids coming out of the city high school system. This vision would in time come to fruition. Immediately after opening the senior citizen center, we raised more than $1.5 million and began construction of the $4 million school. Because of the great demand for the school, in 2004 we doubled its capacity to over 200 square feet.

Some of the people wanted to seek government help. I opposed that. I thought it was perfectly fine to accept government money to build the senior housing, but I wanted this to be the people's school. Today the church subsidizes the school with $40,000 a month, which keeps the tuition affordable.

Once the senior center and school were built, we started building homes. Soon everyone began to look to Greater Allen as the source of turning the prior stories around from negative to positive. But they were not Allen stories; they were *community* stories. Reporters were talking about a church leading the people in turning their own community around. This is how vision becomes reality. The church ought to be the leader in helping to shape a community's vision of what it has the potential to become.

The main lesson here is that vision can begin with opportunity and with the recognition of a need. And vision evolves as new opportunities present themselves. Sometimes the original guiding vision isn't the one that gets achieved first. In retrospect, I can see that the senior housing project laid the foundation for other visions, including the original one.

Ministries start with a vision. Every ministry at Greater Allen is a result of some person's vision to address a need—whether domestic violence, health, troubled youth, or something else. This ought to be the case with any church, regardless of size. Most churches may not be able to start a school or build a housing complex. But each church can be open to receiving and growing a vision in an area and on a scale appropriate to its context and calling.

Consider that with regard to vision, if you think small, you are likely going to be small. Don't be afraid to dream dreams and accept visions that may seem too big to accomplish. "Nothing is impossible with God." Think of yourselves as giants, not as grasshoppers. You have the mind of Christ, so begin to perceive those things that are not yet visible and make them possible by the power of your imagination.

Assessing the Environment

Take the time to develop the unique vision of what God has called your particular church or ministry to be. Too few pastors and church leaders commit to thinking rigorously about the environment in which they are ministering. To develop a vision and a mission, the church must be aware of its identity, both as it is perceived among members and as it is perceived in the community. This will inevitably mean understanding the history of the church and the community of which it is a viable part.

It is especially important for a new pastor to understand what has gone on before. Those who don't clearly understand a church's history may be doomed to be victimized by it. Understanding the past will help the pastor determine whether he or she will have issues to overcome from the past or solid building blocks to move rapidly into plans and programs for the future. Such a fundamental determination could greatly influence the tone of the ministry, especially in the beginning.

The pastor's words to the congregation ought to reflect an understanding of the church's history and identity and perhaps even its struggles. But even if the church has had struggles, dwell on the positives. Let them know that you empathize with their past problems but that you have come to lead them to another level, to greater ministry heights.

Learning and analyzing the church's history should also enable church leaders to determine what, if anything, is unique or distinctive about the local church body. What is its niche? For what is it primarily known in the community? Is it the preaching, the youth ministry, the music program? Is it regarded as a particularly friendly church? Are there flaws that need to be fixed to make the church more appealing to the community?

Environmental assessment entails taking an inventory of all of the resources available to the church. These include church members in various fields of expertise, financial resources, the church's buildings and properties, and relationships or potential relationships with local organizations, including government organizations.

Assessment includes a demographic study of the community. Churches can get the latest data available from the census bureau to determine the demographic makeup of their area. Information, organized by zip code, is available at http://www.census.gov/main/www/cen2000.html.

In addition, pastors and church leaders should attend meetings of the city planning commission and the city council. Speak with council members and other community leaders to discuss future plans for the community. Find out what is being funded. This is the surest indication of their priorities. Once these priorities are determined, the church can begin to consider how it might play a role in the process.

Assessment ought to include a listing of the challenges or obstacles that appear to be standing in the way of the church's ability to accomplish its ministry goals. This may help the church to distinguish between those things it does poorly and those it does well.

The environmental assessment might also include information and analysis about what other churches throughout the nation, particularly successful ones, are doing. This should not interfere with the goal of being distinctive. There is nothing wrong with learning from models that are successful. Simply take the best ideas and try to understand why they are working in another context to determine whether or not they would succeed in your context.

Church leaders should consider devoting a day—or even a weekend retreat—to an overall environmental assessment. This might include inviting some long-time members to share their memories and understanding of the church's strengths and weaknesses as far back as they can remember. (Be sure to tape their testimonies. It will help them understand how truly valuable they are.)

Leaders should then list all the resources they can possibly think of that relate to ministry or potential ministry opportunities. Then they can list all of the challenges and obstacles that stand in the way. The next step is to formulate a plan that removes or works around the obstacles while laying the foundation on which the future ministries will be built.

The assessment process will enable the church to determine which ministry opportunities seem to make the most sense—and which ought to be given the highest priority—given the church's resources and perceived or actual deficiencies.

If the foundation is strong—not built on the "sand" of poor planning because of a lack of proper assessment—you will be able to continue adding to the ministry in degrees you never imagined.

Mission Statements

The primary responsibility of the church, according to Jesus' Great Commission (Matthew 28:16-20; Mark 16:15-18), is to preach, teach, convert, and perform special services to spread the good news of the gospel. Therefore, churches ought not underestimate the importance of a carefully considered mission statement. (See Appendix A.) Developing a mission statement should not be regarded as a mere formality.

It is not possible to build a strong church community without a serious commitment to preaching, teaching, and outreach ministry. Beyond this, a church's mission statement should revolve around the church's distinct identity. How does it see itself as being different from other churches? The goal is not to try to compete with other churches, but to determine the distinctive calling and gifts of the particular, local church in the body of Christ.

A church's mission statement ought not to be "decreed from above." That is, it should not be a product merely of the church's leadership. Rather, all those who participate in the life of the church ought to have an opportunity to express what they believe is unique about the church in which they are active. A simple survey in which members are asked to list (in order of priority) the four or five things that make their church unique is sufficient to gather initial perspectives. The survey could also invite members to write what they think belongs in the mission statement.

After input is received, leadership can begin drafting a mission statement, one that is concise and specific. It should be brief enough for congregation members to commit to memory. And it should be very specific, yet flexible enough to accommodate growth and expansion as new visions emerge. A statement that could easily apply to all or many other churches is not distinctive enough to set the church and its specific mission apart. For instance, the Greater Allen Mission Statement includes education and economic development. These ministries are not an afterthought, but an inclusive part of the holistic mission and reality of the church.

Though it should be concise, the mission statement must be thorough. This means in part that it should not be too narrow or tied exclusively to what happens on Sunday morning. In fact, everything the church envisions for ministry should in some way be incorporated into the mission statement. When people read the mission statement, they should see a snapshot of the church's mission and essential identity.

Rarely does the first draft of a mission statement end up being a final draft. The church leadership ought to have ample opportunity to revise, adjust, and perfect the mission statement. Before the statement is considered final, it should be brought before the congregation for comment and perhaps, based on the church's constitution or polity, a vote.

Remember that the greater the extent to which people are involved in the process, the more they will feel a sense of ownership. For this reason, church leaders ought to promote an atmosphere in which people always feel free to ask questions and give input. In this way, they share in the decision-making process. Church members need to see themselves as the prime players they are as the mission unfolds.

Times change, churches change, and ministry contexts and opportunities change. Thus, the mission statement should be revisited and perhaps reconsidered or reaffirmed periodically. A transition in pastoral leadership is an appropriate time to take another look at the mission statement.

Consider that a mission statement, however well-considered and well-worded, cannot guide the vision of the church if it is "kept under a bushel." Many church leaders would be surprised to know how few of their regular, active members even have knowledge of the church's mission statement, let alone are able to recite or paraphrase it.

A church can do many things to maintain its mission statement—and thus its unique identity—as a focal point in the community. The mission statement, or perhaps an abridged version of it, should appear regularly in the church bulletin or as a part of advertisements for church activities and events. The congregation should recite the mission statement together from time to time. The pastor might, on occasion, use the statement as the basis for a sermon. And it should be analyzed at the annual meeting.

The reason the subhead above is plural (Mission Statements) is that, in addition to the statement that guides the mission of the church as a whole, each individual ministry within the church should be encouraged to develop a statement that encapsulates—again, succinctly and uniquely—the vision for its ministry. This process leads each individual ministry to think within and outside of itself, that is, to consider how the ministry fits within the church's organizational structure and ministry goals. The church's overall mission statement ought to be the standard to which other mission statements adhere.

Mission statements for specific ministries enable these ministries to maintain focus. For example, there was a time at Greater Allen when at each of the meetings of the men's ministry the men were spending most of the time talking about how much fish to buy for the fish fry. There was no mission statement—and no clear vision—for the ministry. Then a mission statement was developed around the goal of building a fellowship that would lead to character growth and development among the men. The mission statement redirected the conversation. Now the men talk about issues of integrity—interacting with their children and wives, what the Bible says about the responsibilities of being a Christian man, home-buying, credit and debt, and much more. They plan retreats and attend men's conferences and other special events. They also sponsor health screenings and career days. Now that they know their mission, they have meaningful experiences.

Constitution and Bylaws
A good constitution and bylaws can be helpful tools that inform people who have questions—perhaps about starting a ministry or addressing an issue—to know whom they should ask. They also help with issues of compliance to the laws of the state and federal governments that apply to churches. (See Appendix B.)

The most important purpose of the constitution and bylaws, however, is to provide a framework for how situations will be managed and how people are to act when potentially fractious issues arise within the church. It is important to keep the constitution and bylaws up to date, especially given the tendency among people in a time of conflict to cite the bylaws legalistically to prove their point. Furthermore, we live in a litigious age. The church constitution and bylaws may be the only thing that saves a church in the event of a court proceeding.

The constitution and bylaws must be vehicles that allow for progress and unity, rather than instruments of division. It is important for them to state exactly what the structure of the organization is in order to prevent unintended results based on technicalities. One of the failures of churches is guidelines (constitution and bylaws) that are not specific enough to address the problems and conflicts that might arise. The result is that some conflicts end up being addressed in an outside legal system that may be insensitive to the realities of the church as a religious organization.

Specifically, the constitution and bylaws should state who has authority in designated areas of the organization. And they should define the process of how this authority is exercised. Periodic additions of articles and amendments may be required to assure conformity to current laws and social sensitivities.

The constitution should also define how the church ministry and programs will move forward. It cannot provide specifics for each situation, but it can establish a general process and understanding that will help to make the rough places smooth. The constitution should, for example, specify how the church defines membership. Does it require regular attendance over a period of time? Does it mean taking orientation classes and being formally received into the church?

As suggested above, the constitution and bylaws ought to outline a process for conflict resolution. In many denominational churches, the constitution and bylaws must be reviewed for conflicts with jurisdictional laws in a particular state.

Finally, given that society is always changing, when creating or revising a church's constitution and bylaws it is important to allow for flexibility that enhances growth. If the bylaws are based on too narrow a mind-set, they could lock out the possibility of the church being able to function in the way that lends itself to a more progressive and successful ministry.

Strategic Planning

The strategic plan determines the church's destination. (The church's budget provides directions for getting to the destination.) Strategic plans should be expansive. Too many churches think about limitations before thinking about possibilities. They know what they would like to do but dwell too long on the reasons it can't be done. At Allen, our strategic plan calls for providing ministry that touches any need a person may have. As a result, new ministries are being birthed on a regular basis.

Any strategic planning ought to begin with a thorough and honest assessment of the church's strengths and weaknesses (as discussed above) and with the church's vision in mind. It should include a listing and evaluation of current programs with a focus on determining which ones are successful, which ones are not, and whether each program ought be changed (and, if so, how). In the business world, company representatives are trained to sell their benefits. Churches should do the same by emphasizing and building upon what they do best.

By and large there are great resources of untapped expertise that exist within our congregations. Many of these people would welcome the opportunity for input. I (Edwin) once addressed a group of ministers regarding community development. Prior to my presentation, the sponsoring organization had made arrangements for a tour of the city. This tour was led by a local person who was a planner for the city. This man knew who owned every piece of property. He was aware of plans and all the timetables for expansion and development. But of the fifteen ministers who attended my presentation, not one had taken the tour, and none were aware of the wonderful resource available to them.

Effective strategic planning should sharpen community resolve with a focus on cooperative progress. Many communities that are being served by African American churches have experienced everything from sustained neglect to active attempts to dump the worst problems in areas populated by minority persons. The problems are exacerbated by a lack of police presence, inadequate social services, and the stigma that the community has very little economic power.

As we develop strategic plans, we need to view our communities and churches not as ants among giants, but as possessors of the land we have been given. Prayerful strategic planning will ensure that the opportunity given by God will not be overlooked and thus the condemnation of Deuteronomy 1:32 and 35 avoided. Here the people were to go into the Promised Land but did not believe God, so God said, "Yet in this thing ye did not believe the LORD your God . . . Surely there shall not one of these men of this evil generation see that good land."

4

The Pastor as Leader

Integrity

THE MOST IMPORTANT ELEMENT OF EFFECTIVE PASTORAL LEADERship is integrity, defined in terms of consistent, faithful Christian living. Integrity must permeate one's personal life, prayer life, and meditative life. It also entails being true to what God has called the pastor to do and be.

The pastor must live and minister with integrity amid all of the pressures of society. The heavy weight of maintaining a high standard is consistent with the recognition that God requires more of us because he has given much to us.

If we are rooted in integrity, it follows that integrity will permeate all aspects of our pastoral ministry and the church's life—preaching, business operations, interaction with the community, and treatment of people, including employees. The pastor who is rooted in integrity, for example, will work diligently to produce sermons that have integrity and for which the pastor accepts accountability. For many pastors, this will mean rising early or staying up late to work on a sermon in advance so that he or she can live with it for three or four days and make adjustments before preaching it on Sunday. People will not come to church for very long if all they are getting fed is leftovers. The pastor should put his or her best effort into producing fresh messages that make a difference in people's lives.

This is not to say that an effective pastoral leader must necessarily be an outstanding preacher. In fact, many are not great preachers but are phenomenal pastors because their integrity draws people to them. Much in the African American church is made of the preaching moment, but it's not just what happens during that thirty to forty minutes in the pulpit that ultimately defines a person as a leader. It's the pastor's integrity that the outside world sees. People will be able to accept a pastor's weaknesses and liabilities—even in the pulpit—if they see an overall image of the pastor that is consistent with their view of a spiritual leader who is living with integrity.

Integrity calls for the pastor to keep the church members informed about the church's vision, where the church is, and where it is headed. This includes financial matters. Keeping people informed about how the church's money is being spent is not only ethical, but it is smart. If you collect money for a long period of time without giving people information, they begin to wonder where it is going, and some will start a whispering campaign that can become deleterious to future fund-raising.

Integrity also requires faithfulness to the commitments the pastor has made. Therefore pastors should be careful about what they promise.

Keep in mind that spiritual leadership that has integrity cannot always be evaluated based on the number of members in the church, though integrity does contribute to gaining and retaining members. Remember also that the church's past and present is fraught with people who wear the garment of spiritual leadership but who lack integrity, love, and the things necessary to build the kingdom of God. Some of them have fallen.

Those who lack integrity might have a tremendous amount of short-term success, but over the long term their inability to build healthy relationships based on integrity will catch up to them. When it does catch up, it is inevitably costly to the pastor, his or her family, and the church.

It is not possible to maintain integrity without understanding that pastors, even as leaders, are followers of Jesus Christ. We sometimes forget this fact because the title "Reverend" or "Bishop" makes us feel like we know everything and don't have to follow anybody. This typically leads to an abuse of authority. Integrity demands that pastors recognize that they are called and chosen.

Attitude and Demeanor

In building the pastoral staff and appointing leaders in the church, the pastor should be careful not to surround himself or herself with "yes people" who will say only what they perceive the pastor wants to hear. You cannot afford to think you know everything. When your head is so big that you cannot listen to anybody, it will lead to problems, especially when you are operating outside your primary areas of expertise.

Not every idea or vision the pastor has will be good. There are times when a vision is good but the timing isn't right. Even if the pastor believes an idea came from God, it ought to be tested with other church leaders. The pastor needs people around him or her who do not feel intimidated, who are not afraid to say, "Perhaps the time is not right," or "Perhaps we should do this a different way," or "We can't afford this now." This does not mean that there is a lack of faith, but that ideas sometimes must be balanced by the judgment and perspectives of others.

That said, however, there are times when a pastor must be bold. Sometimes leadership requires taking an unpopular stand, perhaps even a prophetic stand, even a stand with which the majority disagrees. One example in my ministry stands out. After we built our Christian school, we faced a problem. Directly across the street from the school was a gathering place for alcoholics, drug dealers, and others who represented a negative influence on our children. I believed that one way to get those negative influences out of the community was to control the land.

We had an opportunity to purchase fifteen stores in the block across the street and to develop them as businesses. The trustees, however, voted overwhelmingly against authorizing a $50,000 down payment on the property. They felt that, given that we had just completed a building project, we were trying to do too much too fast.

I was very disappointed. I strongly believed their decision was wrong. Our school for the children was a major investment, and I felt that protecting the children and the building was the right thing to do. So I took the matter to the congregation, telling the people that I believed the Lord had spoken to my spirit with a vision for the property. The women of the church accepted the challenge. They raised the $50,000 for the down payment. In fact, within six months they raised the necessary $300,000 to purchase the property debt-free. We put about $500,000 into renovating the properties, which appraised for $1.4 million. It was a worthwhile investment. We took out $700,000 in equity and purchased more land, which we leased to Jamaica Hospital to build a clinic. We currently collect rent each month on a twenty-year lease.

Taking such a stand is not about running over or intimidating people. It is about doing the right thing. It should be an exception, not the norm. The pastor should not fall into a pattern of always having to have his or her way. But when we feel strongly about something, especially when it benefits others and not ourselves, we must take a stand. That is what effective leaders do.

Pastors should consider that God has placed them where they are for a reason. Instead of just being a pastor where they are, they must learn that real power in ministry is best manifested by pastoring the community and ministering to its needs. There is no need to sit and wait for your next church or the date for when you will become a bishop. A person can't be a leader of many until he or she has proven faithful in overseeing a few. We should be praying, "Lord, bless me right here." It's not about us or our positions and titles. It's about bearing fruit wherever we are.

The pastor should not lead by intimidating others, but neither should the pastor allow himself or herself to be intimidated. It is one thing to care about what others think and another thing to be overly concerned about what they think to the point of being paralyzed by fear.

We minister among struggling, sinful human beings, some of whom will be jealous at what they perceive as the pastor's success. Don't allow such persons to limit the success of your ministry. You are going to be criticized whether you succeed or fail, so you might as well be criticized for being successful.

Sense of Vision

The church as a whole must have a vision, and the pastor ought to convey this vision clearly and consistently. As the leader, the pastor ought also to have a vision for ministry that is related to but is in some ways distinct from the vision of the church. After all, people cannot follow or pursue a vision if there is nothing to follow. The Bible is eminently correct: "Without a vision, the people perish." Not everyone will follow, but if people do not see in their pastor some sense of direction and meaningful purpose, they will be left to drift aimlessly in the wilderness or to find another church.

The pastor's vision might focus on the mission of the church in general or on changing individual lives. It could focus on both, for vision should be multifaceted. People must, however, sense in their spiritual leader a strong sense of mission and purpose and be excited about the same.

The pastor should keep in mind the obvious—that the goal of leadership is to make a difference in people's lives. Martin Luther King Jr. is a classic example of substantive leadership. He understood that something needed to be done to change a system. He developed a strategy, and he invited others into his vision. Andrew Young, John Lewis, Jesse Jackson, and others emerged under King's leadership. We cannot underestimate the importance of reinforcing among the people the goals—the vision—so that they never lose sight of the direction they are going. Nor should we underestimate the importance of encouraging them along the way as Jesus did with his disciples.

Loving the Flock

Many pastors underestimate the association between interpersonal relationships and effective leadership. In fact, some seem to forget that our purpose as pastors is to bring people in, not to run them out! I recommend that pastors, if at all possible, personally greet and speak with staff members daily. Staff meetings are helpful, but they are not substitutes for personal interaction. However, be careful to set appropriate guidelines so that it is clear the relationship between the pastor and co-workers in ministry is based on friendship and professional courtesy.

Ministry, ultimately, is all about people and learning to love people and to love being with and interacting with them. If ministry staff recognizes that you care about them, they will produce at a level way beyond what they will do if they feel intimidated by authority. If you love them, they will accomplish the assigned task and then come back to you and ask, "What else can I do?"

Love must be the basis of our ministry. We are called to help people, some of whom are hurting. They don't need more hurt in their lives, especially if it comes from the person who has been called to minister healing. We should not be opening wounds; we should be the ones who close the wounds and then put salve on them to make sure they heal properly.

In too many instances, pastors don't feel the needs of the people. We should never get so big that we can't feel compassion. We must make it our business to be where the people are, and God will bless us and them. Too often we wait until people have problems before getting interested in their lives. Then it might be too late. Since people tend to sit in the same section, even in larger churches, most pastors notice when someone is missing unexpectedly. Those persons need to hear from their pastor so they know they were missed. Such simple gestures can go a long way toward providing effective pastoral care.

Spiritual Nurturing and Self-Care

One prerequisite to effective leadership is time alone for reflection and relief. Periodic vacations are a necessity. Think about the challenge of preaching. For a person to have something fresh to say to people week after week about where they are today and where they ought to be tomorrow is an awesome task that requires an abundance of time alone with God.

Regardless of the size of the church, a pastor's load can be heavy. In addition to preaching, our role is to be involved in the lives of many people, to celebrate their joys, and to weep with them in their sorrows. This is not even to mention administrative tasks and one's own family responsibilities. To carry this weight requires spending some serious devotional time with the Lord, from whom we will receive the strength and wisdom we need to maintain balance in our lives. Some pastors find a cruise or a visit to the spa to be great getaways.

Every leader ought to have activities or hobbies—something that allows him or her to relax on a regular basis. The pastor must have in his or her life people to confide in, to share struggles and prayer concerns with. Nobody is totally independent. We need someone who functions as a pastor to the pastor, someone with whom we can share anything.

Pastors need people in their lives whose role is to help keep them accountable, to help them see reality as it is, not merely how it is perceived. After all, it is easy for us to get off track listening to our own voices, reading our own press, and listening to people who consistently tell us how wonderful we are.

Finally, we should not underestimate the relationship between the physical and the emotional and spiritual. We are holistic beings; our bodies are temples of the Holy Spirit. Many pastors need to take their physical health and well-being far more seriously than they do. We ought to go in for a physical exam at least once a year. We need to exercise every day and control our weight by replacing unhealthy foods with healthy ones. This is more easily said than done, and given genetic factors, it is far more difficult for some than for others. Nevertheless, this is an area that too many pastors ignore. Even if the results are not as pronounced as we'd like them to be, we all ought to be making some effort to be healthy and physically fit.

Leadership Styles / Models

First, recognize that there is no single, best leadership style. Some leaders are very outgoing, collegial, and gregarious. Others are more internal, reserved. They command respect simply by the way they carry themselves or by the effectiveness of their priestly, pastoral demeanor.

Pastors at both ends of this spectrum—and at all points in between—can be effective as leaders. But the only way for a pastor to be an effective leader is to understand what kind of leader he or she is and then to be that kind of leader consistently. In other words, know who you are, be who you are, and understand who you are in God by virtue of your call. To demonstrate consistent, qualitative leadership, it is imperative that you are secure in knowing who you are. Know your gifts and build on them. Find others to help you in your areas of weakness.

Some leaders lean toward an authoritarian style, according to which all the decisions, ideas, and plans come through them. The risk with this is that the leader will wind up like Moses—burned out—or will drive people out of the church. If you are this type of leader, you need to develop a system that allows you to delegate responsibility to others without feeling that you must be in control or have the final say in everything. This entails finding the best possible people for the right positions and then granting them authority to make decisions and manage in specific, well-defined areas. Delegating will give you more time and energy to focus on what you do best and/or on what you believe is most important. Failing to delegate will likely cause you to have physical, mental, emotional, and even spiritual breakdowns.

Delegating does, however, require time and thought, and it carries with it some challenges and risks. Some pastors find it difficult to relinquish certain responsibilities, especially those of relatively greater importance. They find that worrying about how another person is handling the responsibilities is more stressful than managing things themselves. They prefer to stay on top of everything, and for many this approach works extremely well.

The reality is that, no matter how carefully we delegate, people sometimes make mistakes. Those who opt for a delegating leadership style must have a high level of tolerance as well as a clearly defined process of accountability. For example, if someone makes a mistake, the first time it can be dismissed. If it happens a second time, the leader needs to talk with the person to clarify what the responsibility entails. If it happens again, the leader must take more definitive action. Those who opt for a more authoritarian style are less likely to have to deal with these kinds of problems. However, they will probably get much less done in the long run. Therefore, most pastors, instead of trying to do and control everything themselves, are better off delegating responsibilities and authority to people whose judgment and expertise can be trusted.

Self-Evaluation

Good leaders regularly and consciously look back on various situations and ask such questions as, "What exactly did I do? How did I do it? Why did I do it? What was the impact?" and most important, "What have I learned? How will I handle this differently the next time?"

Too often pastors do not stop to evaluate the impact—both good and bad—they are having as leaders. With reflection and self-evaluation should also come improvement. No fifty-year-old pastor should be functioning in the same way—or making the same mistakes—as he or she was at age thirty. We ought to change, to grow, to learn from every experience. We ought to incorporate new experiences into our ministry activities with the goal of doing better than we did before, of being more effective with respect to the call of supporting people. Furthermore, pastors who want to grow will invite feedback, even criticism, from staff members and people in the pews. An inability to accept any critique is a sign of insecurity. Thus, at the church's regular business meetings, the people ought to have a formal opportunity to air grievances.

Beyond this, the pastor ought to communicate that his or her door is open to those who want to register some concern or complaint. In general, if the church is staff driven, these matters should be referred to the appropriate responsible person. Encourage the complainant to write letters or send e-mails. This forces them to put flesh on their issue and really think about it. This is recommended in spite of the likelihood that the pastor will regularly encounter the same complaints coming from the same people!

Counseling

In this day and age, those on the pastoral staff must proceed very cautiously when it comes to pastoral counseling. This is especially the case with the pastor who has achieved a certain level of public visibility. As much as we want to help people—and as much as we want to think the best about people—we must also be aware that many operate with impure, even hostile or devilish motives. (See also chapter 8, "Legal Issues.")

Claims of sexual harassment against pastors are far more common than they once were. One reason is that some of those who come in for counseling are not in a healthy emotional state. They might "hear" something that was not actually said. Or they might hold the pastor or the church accountable if things do not turn out as hoped.

If the counseling pastor or staff person is not careful, the reputation and ministry of the church can be placed at risk through a lawsuit, unfavorable press coverage, or both. One way to minimize this risk is for pastors who choose to do counseling to have, literally, an open-door policy. That is, the door should always be open at least a crack. And the person being counseled should be aware that the door is open. This reduces the likelihood of the counselee making false claims.

There was a time when pastors could feel comfortable giving advice purely on religious grounds. This is no longer the case. Especially when dealing with deep-seated psychological issues, the overwhelming majority of pastors are neither qualified nor knowledgeable enough to provide the counseling people need. Beyond not wanting to create problems for the church, pastors should want what is best for those we are trying to help. Therefore, it is important to know our limitations and to understand the power of referral. Some churches may have large enough budgets to have certified, professional counselors on staff. Those who do not should develop lists of professionals to whom parishioners, especially those in need of intensive therapy, can be referred.

Premarital counseling is a somewhat different matter. So long as there is no obvious pathology, pastors ought, before marrying a couple, to provide a biblical perspective on marriage and to make sure the couple has considered everything they ought to have considered prior to getting married. When it comes to premarital counseling, churches would do well to take advantage of the wisdom and life experience of laypersons, especially those who have some training in marriage enrichment or marital counseling. At Greater Allen, couples who plan to be married spend about three sessions with four different couples from the church. This enables them to witness marriages from a variety of angles and to hear a variety of perspectives on marriage.

5

Daily Operations

A Professional Environment

AS WITH ANY SUCCESSFUL BUSINESS, THE CHURCH OUGHT TO project an image of friendliness and helpfulness to its constituents. These constituents include the church members, people from the community, and the broader public. More and more businesses are trying to project themselves as being customer-service oriented. Churches ought to do the same. A church with an orientation toward customer service will discover that such an approach is a tremendous evangelistic tool.

Customer-service orientation, stated most simply, means being as courteous and helpful as possible in dealing with those who come into contact with the church by phone or e-mail or in person. With this in mind, churches ought to send some of their staff members to customer-service workshops or seminars.

Churches should maintain consistent office hours. The length of those hours will vary based on the size of the church and its staff, but what is most important here is that the church keep to the office hours that are advertised. Nothing is more frustrating than calling during office hours and getting an answering machine message over and over again.

Don't underestimate the importance of your answering machine greeting. For some, it will be their first impression of the church. Curt, functional messages may come across as being rude. Warm and friendly messages bespeak a church that is—no surprise here—warm and friendly. And of course phone messages or inquiries ought to be returned as promptly as possible.

Effective customer service includes greeting people with a smile. It means maintaining an attitude that says, "I am willing to assist you with your problem." It means helping if we can or pointing people toward those who can help. It means empathizing with others in the situation they are in. Effective customer service is ultimately encapsulated in the Golden Rule—that is, we should treat others as we would like to be treated.

Allen's employee manual includes the following under the subhead "Customer Relations":

The success of Allen A.M.E. Church depends upon the quality of the relationships between Allen A.M.E. Church, our employees, our church members, friends, suppliers and the general public. Our members' impression of Allen A.M.E. Church is greatly formed by the people who serve them. In a sense, regardless of your position, you are Allen A.M.E. Church's ambassador.

Here are several things you should do to demonstrate to members and the general public proper conduct and exceptional service that represents Allen A.M.E. Church:

1. Act competently and deal with people in a courteous and respectful manner.

2. Communicate pleasantly and respectfully with other employees at all times.

3. Follow up on messages and church orders. Provide polite businesslike replies to inquiries, personal and/or confidential concerns and requests, and perform all duties in an orderly manner.

4. Take great pride in your work and enjoy doing your very best to represent the church.

These are some of the building blocks that have been hallmarks for Allen's success. (See Appendix D.)

The Church Meeting

Church meetings, ideally, are opportunities for groups within the church—whether standing organizations or groups formed around a particular activity or event—to better coordinate their efforts for success, however that is defined. Success will result from effective communication of important information and the development and fine-tuning of plans for ministry events and activities.

Unfortunately, too many church meetings degenerate into unfocused gab sessions where little or nothing meaningful is accomplished. In today's busy world, these kinds of meetings will inevitably have a negative effect on recruiting qualified people to serve. In organizing and running an effective church meeting, leaders should consider that, since many of the people who attend the meetings are volunteers who in most instances have worked all day, meetings should be as brief as possible.

CONNECTING WITH THE CHURCH'S MISSION Any subgroup within the church should understand that without its connection to the church, it would merely be an ad hoc committee instead of a ministry. Thus, each meeting of a church organization should keep this connection at the forefront. That is, the group should always have an awareness of how its activities are contributing to the church's overall mission.

One way to assure that the meeting does not lose sight of its ultimate purpose is to have a brief devotional time at the beginning to set the tone and a prayer at the end to send the people forth. Even though brief, this testifies to the group's recognition that its business is ministry.

Furthermore, if the organization sponsors fund-raisers or collects money, this should be reported to the church treasurer. The treasurer then has the responsibility of setting up a voucher system for the organization to draw funds as needed.

AN AGENDA Every meeting should have a clear and detailed agenda, which, if possible, should be circulated a few days prior to the meeting so that people have a chance to come prepared with thoughts and ideas. A well-considered agenda prevents a meeting from getting out of control. If people get off track, an agenda will bring them back into line.

OBJECTIVES To have an objective or objectives for a meeting is not the same as having an agenda. That is, it is possible to follow an agenda perfectly but still not accomplish anything. People can address agenda items without making any firm decisions or definite plans. Those who lead meetings ought to have in mind what they want to accomplish and should guide the meeting accordingly. Progress is necessary if people are to remain involved in the organization's mission.

One common problem with meetings is that they may generate a lot of ideas but no clarity over how the ideas will be carried out. People arrive at the next meeting to discover that the good ideas remain but nothing has been done to fulfill them.

The result is a rehashing of the same things. Again, if no progress is made, people will lose interest.

Meetings might begin with brainstorming, but at some point decisions must be made as to which ideas ought to be given priority in light of the available resources (including human resources) and which either ought to be discarded or put on hold.

Finally, what begins with ideas should end with specific plans. It ought to be clear to the group before leaving the meeting exactly who is going to do what and according to what timetable. If such details are not specified, little if anything will ever be accomplished.

LISTENING The importance of careful listening in a meeting setting cannot be overstated. Most meeting inefficiencies result from the meeting leader not accurately hearing what is being said. Poor listening can lead not only to tangents, but to tension. Good leaders are good listeners.

Listening may seem like a simple act, but doing it well is an art one develops over time. It requires an act of the will to listen carefully while others are speaking and to ask questions if necessary to help clarify their points. Cutting people off and not respecting their opinions and ideas is a sure way of driving them away or making them opponents to anyone else's ideas.

Marketing and Public Relations

The purpose of a marketing or public relations campaign is to get the word out to the community either about the church's ministry in general or about a specific ministry (such as a ministry to AIDS victims and their families) or event (such as a choral concert or fund-raising dinner).

Most churches have limited budgets for such a campaign. Church leaders should consider that most congregations have members who have expertise in marketing and public relations. These people are in a position to lend advice and to analyze, for example, the results of radio or newspaper advertisements. (Obviously, it is important to track these results.) Welcome these members to share their knowledge and creativity.

One general word of advice in this area is that quality is important. In fact, it is probably better not to do anything than to do something poorly, as this can have the opposite of the desired effect.

Churches with limited budgets are usually able to do more in the area of marketing than they may realize. For one thing, they need to take greater advantage of the free public relations opportunities available to them. They should survey the outlets in their neighborhood, taking advantage of their networks and of free public service announcements. Some small publications are regularly looking for copy to fill their community pages, and more churches ought to be providing it for them, especially in cases where churches are addressing issues or problems that affect the entire community.

Public relations is all about building relationships—becoming friends, if you will—with people who, as part of their job, can help to tell the church's story. These relationships will serve churches well, not only in good times but in bad. It is important, if there is negative news coming out of the church, to be honest and candid with reporters who are trusted.

Of course, some churches may need to be on the lookout for reporters or publications that may not have the best interest of the church in mind. At Allen, we have had occasion to deal with reporters who are interested in the bad news but not the good. Over time, church leaders who make an effort to develop relationships with the local media will be glad that they did.

Technology

The days of the manual typewriter are gone forever. Some church people may be afraid of technology, but we live in a technological age, so they need to make the effort to get over their fears. It is impossible to grow a church to the height of its potential without adequate knowledge of the latest computer hardware and software.

All churches ought to maintain a thorough database in order to communicate quickly and efficiently with members via e-mail or letters. Churches—even small ones—should also invest in a website that is attractive, easy to navigate, and kept up to date. Not only is a good website a way to communicate with members, but it is also a marketing tool. We should not under-estimate the number of people these days who are getting their first impression of a church based on its website. We don't want their first impression of the church to be their last one. Allen offers its three Sunday worship services live on the Internet through Streaming Faith. Calls come in from Africa and other parts of the world because of this outreach.

Technology is one of the most effective evangelistic tools available in the world today. It is like "new wine" that cannot exist in "old wine skins." In thinking about getting and staying with the times, churches should be open to engaging young people in technological ministries. They receive from the church, but they also want to contribute. Working with web-sites can be an ideal way to get some of your teenage comput-er whiz kids involved.

6

Managing People

The Pastor's Attitude

EFFECTIVELY MANAGING PEOPLE BEGINS WITH THE RIGHT ATTI-
tude and spirit on the part of the pastor. If a pastor wants the
organization—the church—to be successful, that pastor must
realize that it's not all about him or her.

Pastors who recognize this fact are less likely to become a
"nuclear accident" around which nothing or no one can grow.
Even though it may not come naturally to some, pastors must
make an effort to allow people to grow around them and to
take joy in their growth. We can learn a lesson here from King
Saul in the Old Testament. His greatest failure was an inability
to accept and acknowledge David's conquests.

As mentioned earlier, the pastor should not feel intimidated
by others, but he or she should also take care not to intimidate
others. If the pastor feels threatened, he or she will find it more
difficult to bring to key leadership positions the quality people
the church needs to grow and thrive.

Good pastors keep everything in perspective, work hard, and
praise God for every blessing because they recognize
that ultimately God's power lies behind the church's

accomplishments. Many congregations take on the personality of the pastor, so we must be careful to set the proper tone by acting in a godly manner in all things and at all times. As people witness their pastor giving praise to God, they will be humbler in doing the same.

Delegating Authority

In the section on leadership styles, I pointed out that some pastors tend to do everything themselves while others prefer to delegate. This choice is available to those who serve smaller churches. As a church grows, however, the pastor ultimately has no choice but to share authority and responsibilities.

If, for instance, a church wants to venture into economic development, it needs people with some background in business and finances. Leadership must recognize the difference between a bookkeeper and a certified public accountant. The former might be perfect for a small church but lack the qualifications to serve at a large church that is looking forward and not back. A large church cannot afford to take the risk that the numbers won't add up if the IRS steps in or if a financial institution needs more detailed and complete data.

The senior pastor can feel comfortable delegating authority if the church has been careful to hire competent people. Greater Allen has more than fifty people on its paid staff, but only two report directly to Pastor Floyd Flake and seven report to Pastor Elaine. Bi-weekly meetings and written monthly reports to supervisors are mandatory.

On occasion the pastor will need to defend the decisions of those the church has hired. This can be difficult, especially if someone has made a poor decision. As many organizations, including churches, have learned from experience, even when great care is taken in the hiring process, sometimes the match between church and employee is not exactly one that was formed in heaven.

New Versus Old Talent

Growing churches that are thinking as businesses think are constantly recruiting, even if there is not a current need. That is, they are identifying people who are in a position to advance the ministry of the church and keeping those persons "on file" for a time when the church is in a position to expand or reconfigure its staff.

In seeking new talent, however, churches should be careful not to overlook those who have been with them all along. This can be a dilemma for churches. On the one hand, a church does not want to be too inwardly focused and recruit only from within. On the other hand, there is a trust factor involved in hiring from the outside.

Often a person who has been a part of the body is overlooked because he or she has not been given the opportunity to grow. Such a person may have talents and skills that are advantageous to the church but have gone unnoticed. Thus, it is important to have open discussions with current employees about their hopes and desires to accept greater career responsibilities and adopt new goals.

On the other hand, sometimes recruiting new talent is critical to success and growth. An outside person who has been trained in corporate America, for example, may be able to provide skills that will greatly benefit the church. The right person from the outside can change the character or tone of an office staff, thereby leading to swift change. Decisions must be made on a case-by-case basis as to whether to promote trusted staff or to seek fresh perspectives and approaches from the outside.

Dismissing Employees

My (Edwin's) aunt taught me something very important during the time I worked with her at the local university. She managed the bookstore and had many students who assisted her as part of a work-study program. She is a very warm and generous person, the kind who loves God and people.

One day a young woman came to my aunt in shock after she found out she would no longer be working at the bookstore. She asked my aunt, "Why did you fire me?" My aunt replied, "I didn't fire you. The job did. The job said, 'I have to be done, and you are not doing me.'"

The lesson here is that all church employees, as is the case with employees in any business, have a responsibility to make a contribution that is commensurate with what they are being paid. Making sure this is the case is one aspect of good stewardship. Dismissing an employee need not be a reflection of the employee's character or overall abilities. Often it is more a matter of the person and the job not being an appropriate fit. At other times, of course, some action must be taken because of the employee's lack of competence or character.

No employee of any organization should have to work under the pressure of thinking, "One strike and I'm out." If an employee falls short of fulfilling his or her job description, the pastor or someone else in the church should clearly communicate with the person to make sure he or she understands what went wrong. If it happens again, more communication is necessary. If, however, the problem recurs on a consistent basis, the church, depending on the severity of the behavior, may have no choice but to dismiss the employee. The dismissal of a church employee is one of the hardest challenges most pastors will face, especially if the employee is connected to families or organizations in the church. Unfortunately, many church employees do not take their jobs as seriously as they would in a different corporate setting.

When an employee has to be dismissed, whatever the reason, the situation should be handled with sensitivity, with a pastor's heart, and with concern for the dismissed person's privacy and career future.

Trust Versus Caution

The desire and inclination among pastors and other church leaders is to trust people. However, when it comes to areas involving sensitive information, such as church finances and payroll, it behooves any church to take necessary precautions. As much as we don't like to acknowledge it, not everyone who operates within the church system truly knows and fears the Lord. We are sometimes fooled, and at other times we try to help someone in need by giving him or her a job. That being the case, there is potential for theft or subterfuge.

Some people don't look for opportunities to do anything illegal or immoral but have trouble resisting temptation if such opportunities present themselves. At Allen we have had our share of problems in this area. There is some truth to the saying that locks are for honest people because dishonest people will take anything anyway.

Churches ought to take precautions to ensure that honest people stay honest. This means having checks and balances and accountability systems that make it difficult, if not impossible, for people to succeed at doing something unethical. For example, the church should keep close track of those who have access to various buildings and offices. And certainly more than one person should have knowledge of and access to the church's financial information.

An Employee Manual

As a church grows, it will reach a point at which it needs a clear, thorough policies and personnel manual that describes the church's practices and outlines the expectations both of the church and of the employees. There are many reasons to have such a document. First and foremost, to have in writing clearly defined expectations will result in a smoother and more efficient operation. In addition, a good employee manual is necessary in the event the church is sued by a current or former employee. In the absence of an employee manual, legal decisions will be based not on the church's policies, but on its practices, which in a courtroom setting may be open to debate or interpretation. Not only does a thorough manual serve a church in the event of legal action, but such a manual can go a long way toward preventing legal action in the first place.

Greater Allen's policies and personnel manual is more than sixty pages long. (See Appendix D for an excerpt.) This resource is every bit as thorough as what one would find in a typical corporate setting. It covers virtually all relevant topics, including wages and salary, dress code and appearance, standards of conduct, severance, personal use of church property, sexual harassment, first aid, military leave, and more.

The manual, while stating that an employee's supervisor is continuously evaluating the employee's job performance, calls for a formal performance review once a year sometime during the first half of November. The main purpose of the formal review is to identify employees' strengths and weakness. It is also an opportunity to discuss employees' interests, as well as their future goals and how to achieve them. The end product of a formal review is a document signed by both employee and supervisor. It represents a mutual understanding at the time of the review, something that might be useful in the event of a disagreement between the employee and the church.

Certainly, a good manual must address various worst-case scenarios. Overall, however, it can and should be a positive document. The Greater Allen manual, for example, expresses the hope and belief that all employees will find the church to be a pleasant and supportive place to work. At another point, it invites employees to feel free to express their ideas on how to improve the church's operations. In sum, the purpose of an employee manual is to explain the rules clearly and also to give the employee a positive feeling about the decision he or she has made to become a paid employee of your ministry.

"Term Limits" for Officers

One way to communicate that the church is not about power but rather about ministry is to set term limits on the leadership of various clubs or ministry organizations. Some churches have trouble changing or growing because those who lead key organizations have been in the same position of power for too many years. This works against the goal of getting new people, including young people, involved.

To prevent such fiefdoms, at Greater Allen we instituted a three-year term limit for presidents and leaders of clubs and organizations. (After sitting out at least three years, a past president may run for reelection or be appointed again.) This accomplishes the obvious goal of ensuring new leadership and fresh ideas from time to time. But we have found that it also motivates those who are part of the organization to be more supportive of their leader, because they know the day may come when *they* will have the opportunity to be president.

In some cases, the pastor or pastoral staff should consider appointing, rather than holding elections. This is appropriate especially in cases where people are divided and a contentious election might result in hard feelings. It is also appropriate with groups that are directly related to the effectiveness of worship, such as choirs, stewards and stewardesses, and ushers.

Managing Change

One of the most difficult aspects of managing people is managing change. But if a church desires to grow, it will inevitably have to change. And growth in turn will likely result in many additional changes. Many pastors who grew weary in the fight to change a congregation ultimately gave up and started new ministries that are growing and thriving.

In trying to implement change, it is especially important for church leaders to recognize the importance of relationships. We must treat people with respect and try to get their "buy-in" to new visions. Don't talk to them as if they are children and expect them to respond as adults. With regard to change, this means that we cannot just tell people how things are going to be done from now on. Instead, we need to help them to believe that a new way can work. Meet with them, seek their advice, determine what their fears are, encourage them to believe that they have something to contribute to the growth of the church.

Managing change calls for creativity, deal making, and sometimes compromise. Earlier in my ministry, I had the goal of growing the attendance at the 8:30 a.m. service. I thought this could not happen if I couldn't persuade the choir that sang at the 11:15 a.m. service to sing also at the 8:30 service. They were hesitant to do so because very few people came to the 8:30 service. The people I surveyed in the congregation said they didn't attend the early service because no choir sang.

So I made a deal with the choir. I asked them to make a commitment to sing at the early service for six months, and I committed to preaching. I said that I would meet with them again with the understanding that if they no longer wanted to sing at the early service, I would release them from the commitment. The service grew so fast that in six months attendance exceeded that of the 11:15 service. I met with the choir after that first six months, and they would hear nothing of begging out of the 8:30 service. Today that service is our most popular and my favorite of the three.

We must recognize that not everyone in a growing church is happy about its growth, and sometimes those who are the most unhappy are those we would least expect. Church members, even leaders, may oppose change for any of several reasons. Some simply may have grown comfortable with the way things were, or they may be uncomfortable with sharing power or position. They may not like the new music or being replaced by professional staff.

However, the most common reason for people to resist change, sometimes in direct and subtle ways, is that they feel threatened. Perhaps they feel threatened by the educational credentials of the people who are being brought in to work alongside them or to supervise them. Or maybe they sense that the change threatens to impinge on their positions of power in the church. They do not want to lose control of what has been a part of their domain, even if things can be improved.

The pastor must do his or her best to be sensitive, to understand the feelings and perspectives of these wounded brothers and sisters, even if these persons do not fully understand the dynamics of what is happening. Ultimately, they are not enemies, but friends who are in need of a new perspective and perhaps some encouragement.

When a new person is brought in, persons who have been in the church longer may feel threatened and need to be assured that their experience, ideas, and perspectives are just as valuable as they always have been. Newly hired persons, especially those in supervisory roles, should be encouraged to seek advice and gather information from those who have been around the proverbial block a few times. These practices will help to address many insecurities people may have and will communicate the important message that everyone, ultimately, ought to be on the same side with the best interests of the church's mission and ministries in mind.

Be mindful, however, that some will never accept change and will either leave or stay and fight for things to return to the way they were. They may enlist others who share their views. Sometimes such persons must be rooted out for the good of the church. A divided house cannot succeed.

Recognizing Volunteers

People appreciate recognition. If a church expects to recruit and hold on to good volunteers, it is important to recognize them and show them appreciation on a regular basis. Perhaps after a group of volunteers hosts a conference at the church or coordinates a major event, the church could invite them to enjoy a sit-down dinner. Or perhaps they should be recognized during the Sunday service.

Some churches have a yearly recognition event for church school teachers or other volunteers. There is nothing wrong with this, but churches should also consider recognizing volunteers in a more timely fashion, that is, soon after the completion of their efforts. It makes them feel good about their contribution of time, energy, and resources, and many will hardly be able to wait to be asked again to perform some great task for the church.

Churches should not feel obligated to spend a lot of money for this purpose. An inexpensive piece of art or a simple note from the pastor with just the right message can mean a great deal to a person. Honoring volunteers is yet another opportunity for creativity in ministry. People love working for the kingdom, and they love it even more when their love is sincerely recognized by the church.

Managing "Difficult" People

Managing people entails more than just guiding those on the church staff. It also includes relating both formally and informally with members of the congregation.

Virtually every congregation will have its share of EGR (Extra Grace Required) persons. Some will be more difficult than others. It behooves the pastor to be prayerful and to think of such persons not as troublemakers (though it is tempting to do so), but as people who are struggling in some area of their lives and who from time to time need some extra attention and/or loving care.

Managing people quite obviously requires "people skills." Managing difficult people requires even greater people skills as they relate to basic principles of organizational behavior. Some pastors are more naturally gifted at relating to people, yet any pastor can develop these skills.

Unfortunately, theological seminaries in general do not do a good job in the areas of organizational behavior and development of people skills. Perhaps it is because they presume that "people persons" are born and not made, or maybe they assume that all seminary graduates will become professors.

Although professors need some organizational behavior skills, nothing compares to the skill sets that are essential for successful pastoral ministry.

Pastors and other church leaders can choose positive, productive ways to deal with problems or they can choose negative, unproductive ways. The art of dealing with people starts with the recognition that everybody needs something. The goal is find out what it is. With a little bit of creativity, it is possible to meet the need in a way that keeps almost everyone happy. (Some people's natural proclivity is to be unhappy. That's reality!)

Prior to my beginning a pastorate at a church in Ohio, I had heard about a woman who had been the Sunday school superintendent for more than forty years and was a strong contributor but was likely to make life very difficult for me. I was twenty-three years old but had sense enough to visit her at her house the day after my appointment. She served me tea and told me about how her grandfather and great-grandfather had been lynchpins of the church. I learned that her brother had a drinking problem and was known as the town alcoholic, so I reached out to him at her request and helped him to get his life together. He got saved, gave up alcohol, and became one of my most faithful members.

When the time came to remodel the church, the plan included replacing the altar. Miss Bessie said we could do anything we wanted except touch the altar where her father had knelt. I shared with her my "revelation from God" that we ought to put the altar in the basement, where Miss Bessie had taught Sunday school for forty years, put Miss Bessie's name on it, and make it a permanent memorial in her honor. To be brief, both she and we got what we wanted. She was blessed with an altar with her name, and I was able to lead the congregation in remodeling the church.

7

Managing Money

MONEY PLAYS AN IMPORTANT ROLE IN THE LIVES OF INDIVIDU-
als and families, and also in the life of the church. The acquisition
of financial resources represents some combination of hard work,
creative thought, discipline, and thrift. Thus, a carefully considered budget is essential because it estimates income and expenditures while also prioritizing plans for financial operations.

The spending of money signifies a person's (or a church's)
values and priorities. In fact, someone who knows nothing at
all about a church would be able to describe that church's priorities fairly accurately simply by analyzing its budget and
financial information. Such an analysis might begin by determining whether a majority of members are contributing to the
church financially. Other questions include: Is the church spending money to meet needs in the community in addition to providing for its own upkeep? Is the church spending money on
youth ministry and education? The answers to these questions
and more will be suggested by the general operating budget.

Many churches don't like to talk about money. They don't
like to think about numbers and budgeting. They just want to
"do ministry." We need to move beyond a hesitance to talk

about money, because the reality is that intelligent, informed decisions in the financial arena make a major contribution to the church's ability to "do ministry" more effectively. As suggested above, the financial condition of the church represents what God is doing in the life of the church. If we are afraid to talk about money, we can expect very limited financial giving from the congregation. Growing—becoming more fruitful and productive—will require careful attention to finances.

Lately there have been some negative discussions about the growth of mega-churches. We should recognize, however, that larger churches have the capacity to do more things for their communities. They can afford more professional staff and ministry programs. Regardless of the size of the church, however, it is crucial that members and the community have complete trust in the integrity of the church's financial system. We need to recognize that the resources that come into the church are God's, not ours. And they are to be used for purposes that honor God through ministry. Our role is to be good stewards of God's resources. This requires that we spend the time and energy necessary to understand financial realities as they relate to the ministry of the church.

Being good stewards also requires a commitment to faithfully manage God's financial resources. This means, among other things, that the church's financial systems should include checks and balances to give people confidence in the financial operation. The more confident people are, the more likely they will be to give, which in turn increases the likelihood of ministry growth.

Tithes and Offerings

Historically, tithing has been a point of far greater emphasis in the African American church than it has been in the white church culture. In general, the white church community has had access to many more major contributors than has the black church. For example, when Robert Schuller's Crystal Cathedral was being built, a number of supporters contributed a million or more dollars. In contrast, African American pastors have had to focus on generating resources from a collective body of people. This has led to a heavy emphasis in the African American church on fund-raising events. But it also has meant encouraging people to tithe. From a practical standpoint, in many black communities where churches may be living "hand to mouth," pastors must convince people that giving ten percent is the only way they will see the creation of services and ministries that benefit them. Not emphasizing tithing is a luxury that most black churches cannot afford.

Having said this, however, we must be careful not to preach to our people as if they are all poor, though some, of course, are. Author, speaker, and networking specialist George Fraser said at a recent seminar at Allen that black buying power in America stands at around $800 billion and that with this wealth, African Americans would constitute the world's third largest nation. Though we have the money, we don't always understand how best to use it. An exorbitant amount is spent on consumer goods and other depreciating assets rather than appreciating assets such as homes. Tithes and offerings constitute investments in assets that increase the value and worth of the church while enhancing its ability to assist its members in increasing their own personal assets.

Tithing and Spirituality

More important than the practical ramifications of tithing are its spiritual aspects. Giving to the church is ultimately not about supporting the pastor or giving to the building fund. We give because God has already given us his best gifts—the gifts of abundant and eternal life and of unfailing love. The Bible tells us that where someone's treasure is, that is where his or her heart will be also. By and large, people who have a strong relationship with God express it through giving joyfully and out of thanksgiving for what God has done for them.

Thus, in a very real sense, stewardship begins with raising people's spiritual consciousness. If a church is healthy spiritually, regardless of its size, it will not have issues with finances. For this reason, a church ought to develop a model for teaching stewardship—emphasizing its relationship with spirituality— and should keep this model before the congregation on a regular basis. This principle ought to be incorporated into the new member orientation classes.

Because of the relationship between tithing and spirituality, the church leaders, including the pastor, ought to be tithers. Those in leadership positions must be people who have enough faith in and love for God to give to the church the ten percent that is commanded in Scripture. After all, people cannot effectively teach what they are not practicing.

In teaching and modeling tithing, however, we must be careful to avoid conveying the message that people who give tithes will incur immediate financial gain. Tithing ought not to be portrayed as some magical route to wealth or prosperity. Financial increase requires discipline, faith, and determination. It doesn't happen overnight. Certainly, we need to preach that God will meet the needs of the people, but we shouldn't tell them that they will be rich tomorrow, because this is not likely to happen and it is not because they lack faith or are doing something wrong.

We should also be careful to not put non-tithers in an embarrassing situation. Some churches post the names of people who give, including the amount of the gift. We do not agree with this practice and consider it an invasion of privacy that amounts to spiritual intimidation. If financial records are properly kept, church leaders should be able to peruse them and get a good idea of who is giving. If there is a need to speak to a member regarding the relationship between giving and spiritual health, it should be handled as a private matter. Doing so will enable the pastor to help that person understand the reasons for and benefits of tithing and giving offerings while at the same time providing him or her with words of encouragement and support.

Churches should teach tithing and principles of stewardship on a regular basis. They might also periodically bring in experts in the field to teach on the topic. A guest preacher or teacher may say things that ring true to the listener, who is less likely to consider that the speaker has some sort of vested interest.

The Budgeting Process

A budget is a guide that helps to manage expenses and revenues in the most effective and efficient manner. Budgets should not be viewed merely in terms of cold, hard numbers. As noted, they communicate a church's priorities, but they also present an opportunity to evaluate how that church's priorities are being met.

A budget—whether comprehensive or for a particular event—is a communication tool. Consider, for example, a ministry group that is planning to hold a concert to raise funds. The organizers have calculated expenses for the musicians, advertising, and supplies, and they know what they want to charge for tickets. They have budgeted for 850 people to attend the concert at ten dollars apiece. But records indicate that the previous time a similar concert was held, only 250 people attended. This raises the obvious question of what the group will do differently this time to draw 850 people instead of only 250. This is just one example of how a budget contributes to effective planning. It forces people to talk, exchange ideas, and if necessary, modify plans.

In many ways, the church's budget is similar to a family budget. The goal is to make sure that there is at least as much money coming in (revenue) as there is money going out (expenditures). Churches that want to grow need to have more revenue than expenditures in order to invest in future ministry.

When it comes to budgeting for programs or events, the organizers must consider the goals of the event, including the financial goals. Some events are designed mainly to build fellowship. They might not make any money and might not even break even. Other programs, in addition to serving a ministry function, are expected to raise funds for the ministry. It is especially important for these events to be well coordinated with regard to the numbers and dollars the event is expected to attract. (See Appendix E.)

Budgeting Fundamentals

Many people instinctively think of budgeting only as it relates to planning for the future. However, one cannot plan effectively for the future without first understanding the past, which of course conveys the church's financial position in the present. Thus, the budget ought to consist in part of an organized summary of what the church has done in the past. To do this a church must keep a careful, detailed record of all income and expenditures. Many churches do a good job of tracking this information but do not make effective use of it. Financial officers might not even share it with church leaders. A full understanding of this information on the part of church leaders is a crucial first step in the budgeting process. Many computer-based accounting systems—from the very simple to the very sophisticated—are available to churches to make this tracking process both easy and thorough.

To facilitate tracking expenses, the church should use checks

99.9 percent of the time or more. Churches should use a voucher system or some other process by which designated church leaders can see and approve all expenses in advance. In fact, only certain people should be granted the authority to write checks. In the event of cash expenditures, everyone—the pastor included—should be required to produce receipts for the church's financial officer.

BANK RECONCILIATION As with a family's finances, it is essential for someone to regularly conduct a bank reconciliation, that is, to "balance the checkbook." This ensures that the church's understanding of what it has in its bank account is in line with the bank's understanding, thus guarding against the possibility of overdrafts due to insufficient funds.

Churches should never make the mistake of having the same person who deposits the money and writes the checks do the bank reconciliation. This is a recipe for disaster. No church's financial operations should be under the domain of just one person. For example, someone other than the person who makes the deposits needs to make certain that all of the money that was received on a particular Sunday or at an event is actually deposited in the bank. In addition to protecting against dishonesty, building checks and balances into the financial operations keeps mistakes at a minimum.

CERTIFIED FINANCIAL STATEMENTS All churches should have a trained professional (i.e., a certified public accountant) examine its records at least once a year for the purpose of issuing a certified financial statement. Essentially this amounts to an outside audit to ensure that the church's records are accurate and complete.

Such an audit provides one more layer of protection against inaccuracies or improprieties. It makes the church's financial information visible for all and provides an important document for banks and financial institutions to examine. An external audit must be all inclusive, revealing all revenue, expenses, and assets of the church corporation. If this is not done, it is possible for acts of fraud to be committed, acts known only to the person who committed them. An audit is also a tool to keep anyone, including the pastor, from signing for unauthorized loans—for example, for an automobile—that stand as liabilities against the church. In sum, certified statements represent to members and to the outside world that the church is managing its books with integrity.

Be mindful that if a church aspires to get involved in the area of faith-based initiatives, economic and community development, or other programs associated with government entities and financial institutions, it needs to demonstrate a record of financial responsibility and accountability. This is accomplished only with certified financial statements of revenue and expenses.

REVENUE AND EXPENSE GOALS Obviously, the goal of a church or any other organization that wants to remain on firm financial footing is for revenues to exceed expenses. As for expenses, churches should distinguish between mandatory spending and discretionary spending. Mandatory spending consists of recurring bills that cannot be avoided (mortgage, salaries, utilities, etc.). Discretionary spending might consist of adding new staff or programs or improving physical facilities.

A church can be considered financially healthy and in a position to grow if mandatory expenses consume no more than 80 percent of the church's income. This means that at least 20 percent of the church's income can be spent on current ministry or invested with long-range ministry plans in mind.

This percentage may vary based on the church's needs and goals. For instance, if it is planning to build a new church building or other facility, it should reduce expenses and set aside more resources for the building program. The church may also consider having a special fund-raising campaign directed to a particular project. Remember that if funds are raised for a particular project, it is crucial to use them exclusively for that purpose. This is an issue of honesty and integrity.

If a church's revenues are equal to or less than its expenses, that church can be said to be living "hand to mouth." It needs to take action to address this problem by reducing its monthly expenses, increasing its monthly income, or both. When a church finds itself in such a position, it should be careful not to cut back in areas that will decrease its ministry effectiveness, and, as a result, its opportunity to stabilize or grow. A church that is not serving its people or the community will eventually decline and will likely experience a corresponding decrease in revenues, which will worsen the problem.

Often, creative ways can be found to reduce monthly expenses. These include refinancing the mortgage for a lower interest rate or combining loans to reduce monthly output, even if it means extending the length of the loan. Churches that are struggling financially need to be more diligent in such areas as bidding out contracts for work to be done and not wasting electricity. Furthermore, churches, as with families, must control credit card expenses, perhaps by limiting the number of cards that are distributed.

As for generating income, the church should consider fund-raising events that are consistent with its mission and character and that address a ministry purpose as well. A church-sponsored dinner, for example, can help bring the community together while also raising money. If a church is for the most part empty between Sundays, it might consider renting out space to a local community organization. Churches are one of the very few entities that invest great sums of money in capital building projects and then allow the space to sit vacant during the week.

FINANCES AND THE STRATEGIC PLAN All churches, regardless of in-come, must consider developing a strategic plan. This is especially true for those that are blessed with more income than expenses and thus have the opportunity to carry out the mandates of a strategic plan. Such a plan should be rooted in the church's mission and identity. It should be developed in light of the human and financial resources available or anticipated. The church's strategic plan must also include any opportunities for partnerships the church might form with other churches, community organizations, or government entities and financial institutions.

Among the goals of any church as it develops a strategic plan should be its desire to become a dynamic force within its community. Thus, assuming that twenty percent of a church's income is discretionary, we recommend that half of that (or ten percent of total revenues) be directed toward outreach ministry to the community.

BUDGET PROJECTIONS Drawing up a budget for the future is far from an exact science. It entails analyzing current levels of giving and making a determination as to whether giving will continue at these levels or will increase or decrease. Church leaders must consider any unusual expenses the church might have in the near future, such as a new roof or heating unit. It should also keep in mind the extent to which adding a new staff person will contribute to new ministries, new members, and additional income. There is a saying in the financial world that "you are only as good as your assumptions." This is another way of saying that it is imperative to make projections even in the midst of uncertainty.

In some cases it is appropriate to budget liberally, assuming best-case scenarios with regard to income and expenses. However, many situations will demand more conservative budgeting, especially when there is uncertainty about the income. Regardless of which approach you take, you can be wrong in your projections. In most instances it is probably better to lean toward the safe side with budget projections.

By and large, Greater Allen has leaned toward the liberal end of the budgeting spectrum because it is rare for us not to have increases in income on a month-to-month basis when compared to prior years. We tend to think positively and thus push forward believing that there is much more we could be doing.

Regardless of how a church plans and implements its budget, it ought to remain as flexible as possible in adjusting the budget. That is, a budget that is put in place at the beginning of a church's fiscal year need not be set in stone. The church's leaders ought to compare on a regular basis the financial reality with what has been projected with an eye toward making adjustments along the way. For example, if income is exceeding projections, the church might hire the new staff person it was hesitant to hire three months previously. A church should never take the risk of passing up opportunities if the income indicates that resources will be available for investing in ministry.

Clergy Compensation

Churches should not assume that because the pastor is motivated by ministry they should pay their clergy staff only what they need to get by. The pastor is generally the chief executive officer and should be regarded as such. A church should do its best to pay a fair and reasonable salary, considering fully the pastor's enormous responsibility of leading the congregation both spiritually and administratively. The church's payroll should reflect its sense that all who work in the ministry are entitled to fair compensation commensurate with other professionals in the nonprofit sector. If a church operates businesses and other related corporations, salaries ought to be more akin to those of businesspersons managing similar-sized organizations.

Pastors and other professional staff ought to be compensated based on regular evaluations of their work and its value to the church. In the pastor's case, compensation should include not just salary, but a comprehensive package, including housing and automobile allowances as authorized by Section 107 of the Internal Revenue Code. All employees should be eligible for retirement and health care benefits. Thirty years ago, Allen did not even pay Social Security for its workers. One of my first challenges as pastor was to make the trustees understand that this was not only unlawful but sinful.

Clergy should be paid in accordance with the church's reasonable ability to compensate and in consideration of what is fair with regard to the individual's contribution to the church's ministry. Fairness can be determined based on industry standards, that is, by examining what other churches of similar size are paying their professional staff. Keep in mind that it is not just the compensation that matters, but the spirit in which it is offered. For example, if church officers cannot offer a pastor quite what they feel the pastor's work is worth, they should make sure to communicate this to the pastor. Church officers and pastors alike should strive to make compensation a "win-win" situation.

Determining clergy compensation is no simple task, as each church's situation is unique. However, there are tools available that can help churches determine what is fair for their pastors. One such tool is the annual publication *Compensation in Nonprofit Organizations*, which will be discussed in greater detail later, in the section on staff compensation. (See "Staff Compensation, " p. 78.)

As with the budget, we urge flexibility. So, for example, if a church doubles in size, the officers should recognize that things have changed and should consider whether the change should affect the pastor's compensation package. Of course, things could also change for the worse. If a pastor runs off half the membership and revenues are down, there should be an evaluation that includes frank discussions between the pastor and church officers regarding the direction the church is heading.

However, while compensation packages ought to take into consideration membership and revenue, church leaders should remember that the primary measure of successful leadership is not numbers of people or dollars, but rather whether or not people are growing in their faith. Related to this is the question of whether the church is growing in its capacity to carry out its mission as the body of Christ, as expressed in Matthew 28:18-20. This entails asking questions such as:

- Is there evidence of the power of Christ in the church?
- Is the praise of God a principal emphasis?
- Is the church engaged in outreach?
- Are there new revelations and visions rooted in a relationship with Jesus?
- Is the church actively influencing the community near and far?
- Are lives being changed?
- Is the presence of God the Father, Son, and Holy Ghost evident?

Staff Compensation

Salaries and benefits typically constitute a large portion of a church's budget. When it comes to how much to pay employees, there are no simple approaches or ready-made formulas. In fact, there are numerous considerations, including the nature of the job, the employee's education and experience, and the cost of living in the area or region. The goal is to arrive at an amount that takes into consideration both the needs of the employee and the financial capabilities or limitations of the church.

Salaries collectively represent an investment. Thus, in determining salaries churches must focus not just on the bottom line, but on the question of cost versus worth. In other words, what someone is being paid must be weighed against what he or she is contributing to the ministry. That being the case, it is possible for someone with a salary of $60,000 to be underpaid, while someone making $20,000 is overpaid.

The church is somewhat unique in that the responsibilities of and opportunities for employees typically go beyond what is specified in the job description. Churches ought to consider, for example, that while Mrs. Jones might be only average in her work as a church secretary, she is superlative when it comes to going above and beyond her job description to support and encourage individuals and ministries in the church. Thus, her value to the overall ministry might well exceed the average compensation for a church secretary.

Those in the church who are responsible for compensation should not assume that employees of a church ought to be paid less than the norm simply because they work for a church. Some churches recognize the importance of hiring qualified, credentialed professionals but are hesitant to pay them anything close to the income they can draw in the "outside world." If churches want to attract the most highly qualified people, those with competencies that will truly benefit the church, they must learn to pay them accordingly. The maxim that "you get what you pay for" is more often than not true. When you get someone to work for free or close to it, there are usually quality issues that come into play. On the other hand, when someone is being paid a competitive wage, he or she will have a greater sense of responsibility and accountability to the church's mission.

A comprehensive benefits package—including life insurance, health care, and a retirement plan—should be part of an employee's compensation. It is neither reasonable nor ethical to expect people to work hard serving the church all their lives and then, when they get old, expect them to live on Social Security, which even at its best is for many a paltry sum.

The church may be regarded as a service organization whose purpose is to develop better people. Viewed in this way, in the area of compensation, the church can and should be compared to organizations with similar purposes in the nonprofit arena. Though they go by different names, the job classifications and job descriptions in a church setting often have functional equivalents in the nonprofit sector, equivalents that may be used as benchmarks when it comes to compensation. For example, a church sexton is the functional equivalent of a maintenance worker in the broader arena. The church's financial secretary, depending on his or her skill level, might be comparable to a bookkeeper or an accountant.

Many churches, understandably, wish there were some detailed formulas that would determine exactly what to pay the church secretary, the maintenance person, the music director, and other employees. Because of the many variables involved, such simple formulas do not exist. There are, however, guidelines that can go a long way toward helping churches to determine appropriate ranges for various positions. These guidelines come in the form of nonprofit compensation surveys that consider the nature of the work being done, experience, size of the organization, and geographical area.

Churches with questions related to compensation ought to consider receiving the annual publication *Compensation in Nonprofit Organizations*, published by Abbott, Langer & Associates of Crete, Illinois. In addition to publishing a national edition, the organization publishes editions for several individual states and regions: California, Connecticut, Illinois, Massachusetts, Mid-Atlantic States (The District of Columbia, Delaware, Maryland, and Virginia), New York/New Jersey, Ohio, and Pennsylvania. For more information about this annual resource visit the Web site www.abbott-langer. com/sno.html.

Of course, every position, though similar to others, is in some way unique. Beyond the hard numbers and statistics, various subjective factors enter the picture in influencing compensation in one direction or the other. These factors include attitude, aptitude, long-term potential, spiritual maturity, and work ethic. However, if what a church is paying its employees falls within a range of other, similar organizations, that church can at least feel comfortable that its compensation standards are reasonable.

Perhaps a church cannot afford to pay its employees as much as it would like or as much as they deserve according to the "going rate." If such is the case, all employees should be sharing the burden. It is not fair, for example—assuming there are no extenuating circumstances—for some employees to be compensated at their full market value when others are not.

Churches should look for ways to be creative and flexible in the area of compensation, especially in cases where employees are underpaid. Many church employees, because of the nature of their job description, have to work weekends and evenings. The Saturday evening banquet might not seem like work, but if staff members' presence is required, it *is* work. Churches might give staff members time off during the week to compensate for the weekend time they spend on the job. For fiscal and legal reasons, this process should be documented. For larger churches especially, we recommend a payroll service. A payroll service is an inexpensive way to track employee time and to address the complexities of tax regulations. The reports from the service should be accurately recorded by the church for auditing purposes and as part of its commitment to financial integrity.

While recognizing the importance of consistency, churches ought to allow for some flexibility in their compensation policies in order to reward unusually high performers, those who are making the most significant contributions to the church's business of ministry. Determining when to make exceptions and when to go "by the book" is one of the many challenges faced by those in leadership positions.

We believe that it is especially important to be flexible in the area of church musicians, who in many ways represent a nontraditional job classification. Musicians not only ought to possess unusual skills, but it is also important for them to be anointed persons who have a strong relationship with Christ. Given the realities of supply and demand, it can be very difficult to find quality musicians. Thus, since music is such an integral component of the worship experience, churches ought to be prepared to loosen their purse strings. Excellent musicians may cost from $500 to $1,000 per week, including Sunday and a weekly rehearsal. While this may appear high in terms of the hours spent on the job, musicians' expertise and skill represent many years of training, development, and financial investment.

Keep in mind that from the church's perspective, the growth of the music department is a critical component for long-term success. One director, who is also an organist, understood this very well. He had a beautiful, melodic baritone voice. For years in worship, he had never sung. Then he agreed to do a concert. It was marvelous. Afterwards, I (Edwin) inquired as to why he did not sing more in the services. His humble response was: "My responsibility is to ensure the growth of the music department, and my taking all of the solos would impede that growth."

One model churches might consider is to allow the senior pastor, taking into consideration the church's income, to set the salaries for all staff. (The pastor's salary and benefit package should be set by the church's board or some component thereof.) If the pastor is ultimately responsible for the success and growth of the church, he or she should be given freedom in the area of choosing and compensating a team necessary to implement the church's ministry vision.

Another justification for this approach is that, in most cases, only the pastor works directly with the management team of copastor, assistant pastor, Sunday School superintendent, musical director, and other important participants in the ministry. Thus he or she is in the best position to assess employees' performance. In this scenario, the church board remains responsible for approving the overall budget, and it may also serve in an advisory role in the area of staff compensation. This approach is consistent with the principle of holding the appropriate person responsible for results. On the other hand, board involvement in day-to-day operations is likely to result in confusion and poor decision making.

8

Legal Issues

WE LIVE IN A LITIGIOUS SOCIETY, AND UNFORTUNATELY churches are not exempt from this legal invasiveness. When people feel mistreated or see an opportunity that might benefit them financially, it does not matter that the target is a church. There are also those who have learned to work the system by filing frivolous lawsuits for financial gain, believing that the church will settle out of court rather than risk damage to its reputation. Not everyone who ends up within a church system truly knows the Lord or has the best interests of the church in mind. This is especially the case with larger churches, which are perceived to have substantial financial resources.

A church needs to be careful about any contract it signs. And whenever its physical facilities are used, it should obtain an insurance rider from the lessee. The church should have regular examinations of its physical facilities to make sure they are as safe as possible. This is not only to protect the church from being sued but to protect people from being injured. Most churches have elderly and disabled members; thus churches should make certain that steps and hallways are well lighted and that the legally required supports on steps, on ramps, and in restrooms are installed.

No matter how careful we are, however, things are bound to happen. Therefore, it is important for churches to have liability insurance in the event of a lawsuit. Unfortunately, some who are aware that the church has good insurance are quicker to sue the church, assuming that any payments they receive are covered by the insurance. While this is an accurate assumption, what these people don't realize is that, as with any other type of insurance, when an insurance payment goes out, the premiums go up. Thus, churches should find ways to communicate to members that it is best to avoid lawsuits.

Allen has been sued on a number of occasions, and we have had to learn the hard way how important it is to have qualified and competent legal counsel. The most prominent suit against Allen was filed by a former employee. I didn't worry about it at first because I was certain we had done nothing wrong. Thus, I was convinced the charges would go away. But at some point a lawyer said something to me that totally changed my perspective. He said, "Innocence is not a defense." From that point on, we at Allen recognized the importance of taking very seriously all legal action or threats of legal action, confidence in our innocence notwithstanding.

Proper Precautions

Churches ought to have access to competent legal counsel. Though it is rare to have such persons as part of the paid staff, it is appropriate to have an attorney on retainer. Even in the absence of any legal action, the pastor and appropriate officers should consult with attorneys on a regular basis in order to stay up to date on any changes in the law that affect the church and to assure that the church is in compliance on various legal matters. Among the most recent changes is the legal mandate that anyone who works with children must go through a-background check. (Previously this was advisable but not legally required.)

A detailed employee policies and procedures manual (see "An Employee Manual" on page 58) is also among the precautions churches should take. Clear, detailed policies in writing constitute a solid safeguard against legal action.

Counseling

Those on the pastoral staff are advised to proceed very carefully when it comes to individual counseling. See also "Counseling" on page 43.) In a one-on-one situation, a dispute over an allegation of sexual harassment can end up being one person's word against another's. Again, "innocence is not a defense." Even if a pastor is eventually proven totally innocent, sometimes the damage to the pastor's or church's reputation has already been done, either in the press or on the grapevine. Regardless of the evidence, some will always assume that where there is smoke, there must be at least a little bit of fire. People who have been falsely accused know that such is not the case.

When a pastor assumes the role of counselor, he or she must be careful to establish clear boundaries and have an open-door policy. It is best to stay in the area of spiritual counseling and not drift into areas where he or she is not competent to address the emotional or psychological problems a person might have. A pastor would not attempt to treat someone who has a broken arm or is experiencing heart palpitations, but would send the person to a medical doctor. Similarly, those struggling with deep-seated mental or emotional issues need the help of someone who is trained to address such problems. "Advice" from an unqualified person could do more harm than good. Thus, it could be argued that pastors who do not recognize their incompetence in this area subject themselves to potential lawsuits.

Employment Practices

A church, of course, has the right to discriminate based on its values and goals. For example, when hiring a pastor, a church would not want an avowed atheist in the pulpit. A church may not operate outside the parameters of what is legal. It cannot, for example, fire an employee without reason or cause or pay that employee less than the minimum wage. The good news in this regard is that the laws established by the government have as their goal to respect and protect people. In fact, one could make a strong case that if a church simply follows the dictates of the Bible, that church will be in complete compliance with the federal government.

The situation gets a little more complicated when a church, which is a 501(c)(3) organization, extends itself in other areas. The purpose of the 501(c)(3) is to allow the church to participate in focused ministry while keeping some distance between church and government. Unrelated activities require the establishment of a separate 501(c)(3) organization, which may hire and manage people in the organization based on the organization's stated mission. In some areas, however, there is room for interpretation. It is possible for a church to believe that certain policies are permissible while others think they are not. For this reason, when in doubt, the church must seek more knowledge and information from its lawyers and CPAs.

It is important to be as explicit and thorough as possible with regard to the operating procedures and policies of the subsidiary organization. The laws of our land are not always what believers would like them to be, but we must respect them nonetheless.

9

Community and Economic Development

"Ye are the light of the world. A city that is set on an hill cannot be hid. Neither do men light a candle, and put it under a bushel, but on a candlestick; and it giveth light unto all that are in the house. Let your light so shine before men, that they may see your good works, and glorify your Father which is in heaven."
—Matthew 5:14-16

CHURCHES EXIST IN PART TO MEET THE SPIRITUAL NEEDS OF members. However, a church that does only this might well be considered too self-absorbed and internally directed. The kingdom of God must embrace a much wider and broader mission.

Most healthy, growing churches develop outreach ministries that address the needs of their surrounding communities. In fact, the current political and social climate recognizes the power and leverage of local churches that are intimately involved in their communities, churches whose missions and activities are inextricably intertwined with the lives of the people who are most in need of help.

In a very real sense, a pastor's appointment is not to a church building or congregation, but to *a community*. Most churches will discover a connection between their service to the community and their capacity to grow. As previously noted, people worship where their needs are being met spiritually, emotionally, and economically and where they feel they are being empowered.

The Essence of Ministry

Community development in many ways constitutes the essence of an extended and successful ministry. After all, ministry results from people who, in following God, change first themselves and then their surroundings. This process entails changing how people think about themselves, their lives, and their relationships. There is no more powerful tool for developing a community than changing the quality of the lives of the people in that community.

Community development ultimately begins with having a Sunday morning worship and preaching ministry that powerfully and profoundly addresses every aspect of people's lives so that the people of God have life-changing experiences. When the people of God implement the Word of God, dramatic changes can then take place in a community. The people of God base their actions on a clear purpose and a clarion call for a better life today and tomorrow, and they accept Jesus' commission to "let your light so shine before others, that they may see your good works, and glorify your Father which is in heaven" (Matthew 5:16).

Community Development Defined

Community development can be defined in different ways. It is laying the foundation for growth of the people in a neighborhood in a manner that is visibly manifested. It is exhibiting the joy of the Lord and the power of God in concrete terms. It is the outward demonstration in a broad-based, corporate manner of an inward change.

To conceive of community development in another way, consider a person who has been abusive to a spouse and who changes, or repents, of his or her past. This is a personal transformation. But if that same person participates in, directs, or supports a program that changes others in the neighborhood, he or she is engaged in community development. Thus, community development might be understood in terms of taking a personal transformation to the level of organizing a positive shift in the lives of the people in a neighborhood.

Historically, in virtually every major city, areas that had become majority-minority fell into decline. When the intrinsic value of the location is recognized, the usual plan is to address the underuse (or even abuse) of the neighborhood through gentrification, a word that for many majority-minority communities is a code word for moving the current residents out. The solution for stemming this unjust approach is to become invested in the neighborhood through community development.

Any church, regardless of location or size, has the opportunity to engage in community development. And if just one church takes on the challenge of transforming the people in the neighborhood, there will most likely be a shift in the attitude with which people view the neighborhood and the relationship they have with its residents.

When several churches contribute to this effort, the potential for change is enormous. Investing in a community tends to attract the attention and support of others who want to be a part of making a difference. Soon a neighborhood that was seen as being in decline is viewed as a vibrant and growing place in which people believe and are willing to invest.

Home and Land Ownership

In striving for community development, many African American churches underestimate the importance of home ownership. According to the Fannie Mae Foundation, only 48 percent of African Americans live in homes they own as compared to over 75 percent of white America.

A home is an appreciating asset. It is very difficult to build a stable community—including a stable church community—with a renting population. Ownership stabilizes families and communities. With home ownership comes power and the foundation for prosperity through equity. Renters, after all, are under someone else's control. The greatest support program available to every person in the country is the tax deductibility on home mortgages. In effect, the government subsidizes homeowners. By virtue of its policies, the government partners with every homeowner in building wealth, in giving people the opportunity to acquire assets that more often than not grow to become greater than their liabilities.

Related to homeownership is the purchasing and development of land. One of the realities of many urban areas is the vast blocks of land that lie vacant. In some cases, there is nothing on this land but weeds and broken glass. Sometimes there are dilapidated buildings. Typically this land is owned by the city, which acquired it as people became too poor or too old to pay property taxes.

The migration of the middle class, both white and black, out of urban areas left behind many vacant properties. Churches should realize that government authorities, politicians, and community leaders all have a vested interest in seeing this land developed in ways that contribute to the welfare and growth of the community. This is a perfect opportunity for a church to provide ministry to the community by setting up community development corporations (CDCs). Churches—and individuals for that matter—would be much better off investing in land than in, for example, the stock market. As with homes, real estate is almost invariably an appreciating asset.

In 1976 Allen developed a federal government–sponsored Section 202 senior citizen housing project. In accordance with this project, we were able to purchase several acres of land in Queens, New York, from the city. The city trusted us because by then we had developed a solid track record for making use of the land we owned.

As of the publication of this book, Greater Allen has built more than 160 new homes from the ground up. In building housing, it is important to keep in mind how large a monthly mortgage people will be able to afford. One way we addressed this issue was by building two-family homes with a rental unit in each house. Thus, a good portion of the monthly mortgage is paid by the renter. It is a win-win situation for the owner, who receives income while building equity.

Too many organizations with the purest of motives focus on building housing for those at the lowest income levels. While churches ought not to ignore the needs of low-income families, to build housing that puts all low-income persons in one place is in essence to build a future ghetto. It is important to have balance, and this goal is achieved by making sure there are people of mixed incomes—many of whom are taxpayers—in the neighborhood.

Investing in Community Development

Community development requires a tremendous amount of time and effort. For many churches, the process of identifying community needs is relatively easy, because in many majority-minority communities there is a dearth of services and programs. However, noticing a need is not the same as recognizing an opportunity. Many times churches have opportunities right at their front door but fail to take advantage until gentrification begins. By then it may be too late.

Initially, a portion of the pastor's (and leadership's) time should be allocated to laying the groundwork of a development project. It will likely be a while before the church is able to hire staff to oversee this effort. Until then, community development work can seem like a full-time job to the pastor. Bringing a vision to reality requires prayer and work. It also requires that the pastor get out of the office. Copastor Elaine Flake spent time at the state Department of Education and other government offices so that when it came time for us to build a school, all of the legal requirements were met.

Church community development can be organized around three basic principles—the three Es of community development ministry: expectation, exposure, and experience.

EXPECTATION Expectation is the ability to believe that a vision can become reality when implemented through an administrative process. It calls for putting feet to faith, looking at the steps necessary to move from the current condition to the place God is attempting to take you. One must have faith and work diligently so that the search for resources will be successful. Expectation does not take no for an answer. Expectations walk by faith and abide by God's timing. Expectations, therefore, are active.

I (Edwin) once met with two pastors who fully exemplified the attitude of expectation. They have a small church that is living a large vision. Several years ago, they purchased a piece of property in Manhattan. When they began, they had $5,000 for the land, for which the asking price was over $400,000. When they went to a lawyer, he refused to discuss the transaction. Within two months they had accumulated an additional $20,000. They found a new attorney, who also informed them that this amount was insufficient. However, this attorney was willing to work with them. He indicated that they would need at least $150,000 as a down payment.

With expectation and faith, the church continued to raise the necessary funds. The attorney arranged for a loan from a private source for $250,000, using the credit of church members. This is reminiscent of the financing of many African American churches and schools. The people of God had expectations that having a house of worship would have a meaningful impact on their lives. Therefore they were willing to risk their homes and farms for the vision, based on the expectation that a church facility would make a significant difference in their own lives and in the life of the community.

A church must be open to any possibility that is consistent with its theological focus, priorities, and vision. Greater Allen had no initial plans for a ministry focusing on domestic violence, but when the city invited us to consider it because we had available space, we did. As a result, our Women's Center has now been in place for more than twenty years.

EXPOSURE Exposure means becoming aware of available resources and beginning to establish a reputation for the church and its leadership. Exposure can be quiet. It need not mean media coverage. Rather, it comes from working hard and from making partners of others so that they become participants in the future success.

Exposure, in part, entails a process of building relationships. All programs and all community development is ultimately personal. During the first six years at Greater Allen, Pastor Flake spent a day each week in Manhattan visiting the offices of Housing and Urban Development (HUD), the city real estate department, human resources agencies, and other organizations, and spent time asking questions and getting to know people.

Exposure means being aware of opportunities. Read every local paper each day, paying particular attention to notification of each upcoming Request For Proposals (RFP), which are in essence invitations from government entities to accept bids on various development projects. To help your community, you must know something about the direction of city, state, and even national policies. Ask about new programs that will help in implementing the vision. Build a wide array of contacts and keep expanding them.

Exposure also means developing partnerships. Community development does not happen in a vacuum. Every project involves the components of a business with a focus on the measurement of results. For any project, one must first determine who is the consumer or customer. Who will be the recipients of the community development effort? Who needs the health care, and where are they being served now? How much will the church be able to fund, and is this amount sufficient to successfully complete the project?

The church, or its subsidiary corporation(s), is in essence in partnership with the consumers to deliver an appropriate product for the neighborhood. It must therefore ask, What are the track records of potential partners in implementing the program? What are the objectives of the builder or of the funding sources?

Does the church understand the partnership arrangement? Every person and organization involved in the development process is a partner: the architect, the appraiser, the engineer, the construction contractor, the insurance broker, the real estate agent, the project manager for the funding source, the financial institution, the politicians, and others. All of these partners ought to be pursuing the goal of delivering services at or below the market cost while at the same time changing the community for the better.

Exposure has allowed Greater Allen to reach a point at which local authorities call us if they are aware of a project in which we might be interested. For example, we were approached to take part in an effort to promote abstinence, which resulted in our K.E.P.T. (Keep Every Person True) program. Arriving at this point does not happen overnight. For most churches, there will be a season of hard work accompanied by much disappointment and discouragement. Many banks will turn you down at first, but those who persevere in the strength of the Lord will be rewarded for their striving.

EXPERIENCE Experience is the third component critical to success. With each new project, the experience of the past must be brought to the table so that the church does not start from the low end on the learning curve. For example, experience is valuable when completing a HUD senior citizen housing application, for it is a complex and arduous process that very few people can successfully navigate. Moreover, stress is compounded by the limited time the funding source has to educate a new group about the nuances associated with the process. Experience, however, informs applicants of the importance of hiring a competent consultant, a person who can navigate the waters for a successful submission. Experience teaches a church to research the most successful consultants by reviewing previously approved programs as well as by talking to others who have created similar community development programs.

Many beginning organizations struggle longer than necessary because they will not seek the expertise they need. Some hold the mistaken belief that getting assistance in some way diminishes what has been accomplished. Instead, they should view those people with expertise as important partners in the process. Their experience will shorten the time it takes to implement a successful program.

Government Requirements

If a church is to provide services to the community, it must be prepared to abide by government requirements even if they seem cumbersome. We need to avoid the temptation to allege racist motives when demands are made to produce more documents or information or to make changes. For example, when we were preparing to launch a daycare facility, one of the requirements was to put children's toilets in the building. We had to convince some who felt burdened by this requirement that there was nothing racial about installing toilets for little children if we were going to have a daycare for which the clients would be little children.

Churches are well advised to form a separate nonprofit corporation when seeking to enter a partnership arrangement using government funds. The nonprofit corporation is known as a 501(c)(3), a designation based on the section of the IRS code in which such organizations are described. A 501(c)(3) is a tax-exempt corporation whose purpose is to serve the public good. The link for filing an application is http://www.irs.gov/publications/p557/ar01.html. The link for churches is http://www.irs.gov/pub/irs-pdf/p1828.pdf. A 501(c)(3) provides some distance between church and government. If government money is coming directly to the church, there is a risk of the state getting too involved in the life of the church.

Establishing a 501(c)(3) requires forming a board of directors, setting a budget, and adopting a mission statement and bylaws. Once these are approved by the IRS, the organization will receive a tax-exempt number and can then receive government funds. Although applications are available from the IRS, churches are advised to enlist an attorney in the process.

In forming the board, the church should focus on persons who clearly understand the relationship between the church and the nonprofit organization. The nonprofit is a separate entity for legal purposes, but it is not unrelated to the church. Effectively organized nonprofits share a vision for ministry that is the same as or that complements the vision of the church.

There are two very different basic approaches to forming a nonprofit board. One is to build it internally by choosing people from the governing board of the church. This approach ensures that the policies and goals of the two organizations will be consistent, resulting in the kind of synergy between the organizations that maximizes potential. Though some church members might feel that serving on the board of a community organization is a bit daunting, in general good church officers should make for good board members.

An alternative board structure is to solicit high-profile individuals outside the church, people who bring some expertise and can provide not only financial support to the nonprofit organization, but also the kind of stature that enhances the organization's credibility, thus improving its prospects for attracting resources. The risk is that some visible leaders will use the organization to enhance their own purposes. Some people serve on the boards of so many organizations that it is impossible for them to make a meaningful contribution to any of them.

Combining these two alternative approaches is also an option. In selecting people from outside the church, one important criterion is that the persons have some degree of expertise related to the specific mission or purpose of the nonprofit organization so that they can provide meaningful guidance.

Ultimately, everything that happens in both organizations must be true to the mission of the church. Its name and reputation are at stake. However, the specific activities of the nonprofit organization, by law, must be limited to what is specified by the mission statement. So if the purpose of the organization is to feed the hungry, the corporation may not, for example, make gospel messages a part of its agenda.

These limitations make some churches hesitant to accept government money, even though the limitations apply only to the nonprofit organization. Churches that are struggling in this area might do well to recall the words of St. Francis of Assisi: "Preach the gospel at all times and, when necessary, use words."

Churches might view nonprofit organizations as vehicles through which to demonstrate God's love, as opposed to proclaiming it. The reality is that many of those who are served by the nonprofit organization will end up going to the church with which the service organization is associated. The current political emphasis on faith-based initiatives has by and large allowed churches to make use of government money without many cumbersome strings attached.

Networking and Deal Making

Pastors must approach community development with a mindset that is constantly considering resources, possibilities, and potential partnerships. Often the resources are closer than we realize. For example, several years ago the leaders of Greater

Allen had a vision to provide quality home care to the community. We knew the city would fund it, but we had so many other things going on that we felt overwhelmed. Then we found out about a young woman from the church who was traveling from Queens to Harlem every day to run a home care program. We enlisted her to write the proposal. She has directed our home care program for more than two decades now.

When it comes to forming relationships with business, political, and community leaders, pastors need to be as extroverted as their personalities will allow them to be. As Rev. Reed puts it, "We shouldn't be showing up at receptions just to eat the hors d'oeuvres."

Mastering the art of the deal begins with putting together a good team. And putting together a good team begins with research. You will likely discover, as we did, that a high percentage of funded projects get awarded to a relative handful of people. Find out who those consultants and builders with a successful track record are and get them on your team. Get to know the people in your local HUD offices as well as other city and state officials. Use the Internet, the greatest equalizing factor of our generation, to find out what opportunities are available.

As with many things in life, the hardest part might be getting an opportunity to prove yourself. When that happens, remember that everyone wants to look good in the end, including the local HUD officials, the mayor, the builder, and the bank.

Thinking Politically

In forming and developing relationships with government leaders, churches do well to think practically in terms of the goals they are trying to accomplish. Specifically, this means among other things that you should not be beholden to one political party or another. For churches doing community development, there ought not to be liberals or conservatives, Republicans or Democrats. The best way to maintain your principles is to continue to "speak truth to power," but it is also important to make that power work for you. Politics controls the land and zoning regulations, thus it is important to think strategically.

To accomplish community and economic development goals, church leaders need to be present at the table (sometimes literally). We need to be building relationships with political leaders of all stripes to ensure a positive relationship with whoever is elected. This might mean attending a dinner for one candidate one month and another dinner for his or her opponent the next month. That's what successful businesspeople do.

Some criticize this approach, considering it a compromise of principles. Our response is that principles need to be weighed against one another. Getting the most you can for your community is also an important and worthy principle.

On the topic of thinking practically, too many African American churches won't proceed unless they have a black architect and black builders. We at Allen have as much black pride as anyone, but the main goal is to meet the needs of the congregation and the community. That means we will find the people who will finish the building with quality workmanship within the allotted budget and on time.

The Language of Business

When churches are operating in the secular arena, they need to step away from "God language." Government and financial institutions do not understand "God language," nor should we expect them to. These institutions want to deal with the church as a business. Develop a church business plan, pray about it, and know that God will be better able to answer your prayer if you have a plan.

Sometimes it is difficult for secular organizations to consider the church as a business. When we sought a $17 million loan to build our new cathedral, the bank initially turned us down. We had reliable projections of how much our revenue would increase at each of our three services if we could seat more people, but the bank had never before loaned that amount of money to a church. The bank officials acknowledged that if they saw the same revenue projections coming from a small business, they would not hesitate to grant the loan. Rev. Reed was able to change their perspective—from viewing Allen as a church to viewing us as a small business.

Today the offerings from just the first Sunday of each month are more than enough to cover the mortgage payment. The moral of this anecdote is "Don't quit." If you have reliable revenue projections based on certified financial statements, fairness and rationality are ultimately on your side.

Some in the church have trouble thinking of the church as a business. As stated earlier, however, we need to think of ourselves as being in the business of doing ministry. Generating income and using it responsibly increases our capacity to do effective ministry. Let us not forget that everything God has given to others he has also given to us.

Many churches can do more than they realize in the area of generating income. For example, why allow weddings to go outside the church? Perhaps some relatively small investments to the physical facility could make the church more attractive— even elegant—for weddings and receptions. At least some of the money saved (usually by the bride's parents) is likely to be given to the church as a gift of appreciation.

As suggested above, purchasing and developing land ought

to be a viable option for churches to generate income. Greater Allen has benefited greatly from stores paying rental income.

Economic Development

The second stage of community development is economic development, which may be defined as organizing business enterprises that provide goods and services to the community in response to market needs. Unlike the typical community development venture, economic development does not depend on donated funds. In fact, very little institutional funding goes into businesses.

Economic development is successful to the extent that a market need is identified and addressed in such a way that people are willing to pay for whatever goods or services the business is providing. With the successful creation of business ventures, communities have access to a greater tax base, which in turn is likely to lead to more economic growth and better public services.

At Greater Allen, economic development is best exemplified by Allen Transportation, which began in 1987 with the purchase of three buses. It is now a full-service bus operation with six fifty-five-passenger scenic cruiser vehicles providing charter transportation throughout the East Coast.

Churches must be aware that, with profit-making corporations, the rules are the same as with any other business. A church, for example, can choose to hire only persons of religious faith, whereas a profit-making corporation may not discriminate in that way.

In considering starting a business, the church needs to do what every other business does, which is to assess needs and determine which goods or services are likely to make a profit.

Churches should consider how likely their members are to support the business. In the case of Allen Transportation, church members constitute a significant portion of the clientele. That is, many church members had already been taking bus trips. Now the profits remain with the church instead of going to an outside company. Allen Transportation is wholly owned by Allen A.M.E. Church, so the church benefits from its profits.

Venturing into the areas of community and economic development is not easy. It requires a great deal of work, patience, creativity, networking, and risk taking. Churches should begin by building quality ministries in the church. A solid educational ministry might be a perfect foundation for an after-school program.

Don't believe that nothing can be done just because everything can't be done simultaneously. Greater Allen grew to the prominence it has today not overnight, but one step—one new project—at a time. Be encouraged. Trust God. Have faith when there is a sense that the Lord is leading the vision. "Where there is no vision, the people perish" (Proverbs 29:18).

APPENDIX A

Sample
Mission Statement

IT IS THE MISSION OF THE GREATER ALLEN A.M.E. CATHEDRAL OF New York to effectively minister the Word of God to the people of God through teaching, preaching, and outreach. We believe that we are called to address the needs of the total person, as our Savior did, and strive to lift the name of Jesus in our community and the world in which we live through our commitment to praise, worship, stewardship, evangelism, and economic development.

Sample Constitution and Bylaws

CONSTITUTION

PREAMBLE

WE DO DECLARE AND ESTABLISH THIS CONSTITUTION TO PRESERVE AND secure the principles of our faith and to govern the body in an orderly manner. This Constitution will preserve the liberties of each individual church member and the freedom of action of this body of immersed believers in relation to other churches.

I. NAME

This body shall be known as _____(name of Church) with a mailing address of _____(mailing address).

II. PURPOSE

To share Christ with as many people as possible through witnessing and mission outreach; to be a church that ministers unselfishly in our community and to be involved in the betterment of that community; to aid as we are able; to bring relief to those who are in bondage to poverty, ignorance, fear, prejudice, or hostility.

III. ARTICLES OF FAITH

1. We believe that the Holy Bible was written by people who were divinely inspired and is a perfect treasure of heavenly instruction; that it has God for its Author, salvation for its end, and truth without any mixture of error for its matter; that it reveals the principles by which God will judge us, and therefore is, and shall remain to the end of the world, the true center of Christian union and the supreme standard by which all human conduct, creeds, and opinions shall be tried.

2. We believe the Scriptures teach that there is one, and only one, living and true God, an infinite, intelligent Spirit, whose name is Jehovah, the Maker and Supreme ruler of heaven and earth; inexpressibly glorious in holiness, and worthy of all possible honor, confidence, and love; that in the unity of the Godhead there are three persons—the Father, the Son, and the Holy Ghost, equal in every divine perfection, and executing distinct but harmonious offices in the great work of redemption.

3. We believe the Scriptures teach that humankind was created in holiness, but by voluntary transgressions fell from that holy and happy state; in consequence of which all human beings are now sinners, not by constraint but choice; being by nature utterly void of that holiness required by the law of God, positively inclined to evil; and therefore under just condemnation to eternal ruin, without defense or excuse.

4. We believe that the Scriptures teach that the salvation of sinners is wholly of grace: through the mediatorial offices of the Son of God, who by the appointment of the Father freely took upon Him our nature, yet without sin; honored the divine law by his personal obedience, and by His death made a full atonement for our sins; that having risen from the dead, He is enthroned in heaven; and uniting in His wonderful person the most tender sympathies with divine perfection, He is in every way qualified to be a suitable, a compassionate, and all sufficient Savior.

5. We believe the Scriptures teach that the great Gospel blessing, which Christ secures to such as believe in Him is justification; that includes the pardon of sin, and the promise of eternal life on principles of righteousness; that it is bestowed, not in consideration of any works of righteousness which we have done, but solely through faith in the Redeemer's blood; by virtue of which faith His perfect righteousness is freely imputed to us of God; that it brings us into a state of most blessed peace and favor with God and secures every other blessing needful for time and eternity.

6. We believe that the Scriptures teach that the blessings of salvation are made free to all by the Gospel; that it is the immediate duty of all to accept them by cordial, penitent, and obedient faith; and that nothing prevents the salvation of the greatest sinner on earth, but his or her own determined depravity and voluntary rejection of the Gospel; which rejection involves him or her in an aggravated condemnation.

7. We believe that the Scriptures teach that in order to be saved, sinners must be regenerated, or born again; that regeneration consists in giving a holy disposition to the mind that it is affected in a manner above our comprehension by the power of the Holy Spirit in connection with divine truth, so as to secure our voluntary obedience to the Gospel; and that its proper evidence appears in the holy fruits of repentance and faith, and newness of Life.

8. We believe the Scriptures teach that repentance and faith are sacred duties, and also inseparable graces, wrought in our souls by the regenerating Spirit of God; whereby being deeply convinced of our guilt, danger, and helplessness and of the way of salvation by Christ, we turn to God with unfeigned contrition, confession, and supplication for mercy; at that same time heartily receiving the Lord Jesus Christ as our prophet, priest, and king, and relying on Him alone as the only and all-sufficient Savior.

9. We believe the Scriptures teach that election is the eternal purpose of God, according to which He graciously regenerates, sanctifies and saves sinners; that being perfectly consistent with the free agency of humankind, it comprehends all the means in connection with the end; that it is a most glorious display of God's sovereign goodness, being infinitely free, wise, holy, and unchangeable; that it utterly excludes boasting and promotes humility, love, prayer, praise, trust in God, and active imitation of His free mercy; that it may be ascertained by its effects in all who truly believe the Gospel; that it is the foundation of Christian assurance; and that to ascertain it with regard to ourselves demands and deserves the utmost diligence.

10. We believe the Scriptures teach that Sanctification is the process by which, according to the will of God, we are made partakers of His holiness; that it is a progressive work; that it is begun in regeneration; and that it is carried on in the hearts of believers by the presence and power of the Holy Spirit, the Sealer and Comforter, in the continual use of the appointed means especially the word of God, self-examination, self-denial, watchfulness, and prayer.

11. We believe the Scriptures teach that such only are real believers as endure to the end; that their persevering attachment to Christ is the grand mark which distinguishes them from superficial professors; that a special Providence watches over their welfare; and they are kept by the power of God through faith unto salvation.

12. We believe the Scriptures teach that the Law of God is the eternal rule of His moral government—that it is holy, just, and good; and that the inability which the Scriptures ascribe to fallen persons to fulfill its precepts results entirely from their love of sin.

13. We believe the Scriptures teach that a visible church of Christ is a congregation of baptized believers, associated by covenant in the faith and fellowship of the Gospel; observing the ordinances of Christ; governed by His laws; and exercising the gifts, rights, and privileges invested in them by His Word; that its only scriptural officers are Bishops or Pastors, and Deacons, whose qualifications, claims, and duties are defined in the Epistles to Timothy and Titus.

14. We believe the Scriptures teach that Christian baptism is the immersion in water of a believer, into the name of the Father, and Son, and Holy Ghost; to show forth in a solemn and beautiful emblem, our faith in the crucified, buried, and risen Savior, with its effect, in our death to sin and resurrection to a new life; that is prerequisite to the privileges of a church relation; and to the Lord's Supper, in which the members of the church, by the sacred use of bread and wine, are to commemorate together the dying love of Christ, preceded always by solemn self-examination.

15. We believe the Scriptures teach that the first day of the week is the Lord's Day, or Christian Sabbath, and is to be kept sacred to religious purposes, by abstaining from all secular labor and sinful recreations, by the devout observance of all the means of grace, both private and public, and by preparation for that rest that remains for the people of God.

16. We believe the Scriptures teach that civil government is of divine appointment, for the interest and good order of human society; and that magistrates are to be prayed for, conscientiously honored, and obeyed; except only in things opposed to the will of our Lord Jesus Christ, who is the only Lord of the conscience, and the Prince of the Kings of the earth.

17. We believe the Scriptures teach that there is a radical and essential difference between the righteous and the wicked; that such only as through faith are justified in the name of the Lord Jesus, and sanctified by the Spirit of our God, are truly righteous in His esteem; while all such as continue in impenitence and unbelief are in His sight wicked, and under the curse; and this distinction holds among humankind both in and after death.

18. We believe the Scriptures teach that the end of the world is approaching; that at the last, Christ will descend from heaven and raise the dead from the grave for final retribution; that a solemn separation will then take place; that the wicked will be adjudged to endless punishment, and the righteous to endless joy; and that this judgment will fix forever the final state of men and women in heaven or hell, on principles of righteousness.

IV. COVENANT

Having committed ourselves to the Lord Jesus Christ, experiencing the mercy, forgiveness, and redemption of God our Father, and of the Son and of the Holy Spirit, we do now in the presence of God and this assembly, covenant with one another as members of _____(name of church) Church, as one body in Christ. We do therefore, with God's help, through the guiding presence of the Holy Spirit engage to walk together in Christian love, sharing one another's joys and bearing one another's burdens; to counsel, admonish, and encourage one another; to assemble faithfully in the name of Jesus for worship, study, and fellowship; to pray earnestly for others as well as for ourselves; to strive for the advancement of this church in knowledge, holiness, and comfort; to promote its prosperity and spirituality; and to sustain its worship, ordinances, discipline, and doctrine; to contribute cheerfully and regularly, as God has prospered us, to the support of the ministry and expenses of the church; to faithfully and willingly give of our time and talent to fulfill the mission of this church; and to be faithful stewards of all God has entrusted to us; to engage in secret and family prayer; to bring up those in our care in the nature and admonition of the Lord.

Further, we will seek, by Christian example and personal witness, to win others to Christ and encourage their growth toward Christian maturity; to prove the reality of our spiritual conversion by abstaining from conduct unbecoming to a Christian and contrary to the teachings of Christ; and by striving to uphold the high standards of Christian morality.

We also promise that when we remove from this vicinity we will, as soon as possible, unite with some other church where we can carry out the spirit of this covenant, and the principles of God's Word, striving always to live to the glory of the One who has called us out of darkness into God's marvelous light.

V. POLICY

The government of this church is vested in the members who compose it. Persons duly received by the members shall constitute the membership.

All internal groups created and empowered by the church shall report to and be accountable only to the church unless otherwise specified by church action.

This church is subject to the control of no other ecclesiastical body, but it recognizes and sustains the obligations of mutual counsel and cooperation, with other Christ-centered churches.

BYLAWS

I. CHURCH MEMBERSHIP

SECTION 1. General

This is a sovereign and democratic Baptist church under the Lordship of Jesus Christ. The membership retains unto itself the exclusive right of self-government in all phases of the spiritual and temporal life of this church.

The membership reserves the exclusive right to determine who shall be members of this church and the conditions of such membership.

SECTION 2. Candidacy

Any person may offer himself or herself as a candidate for membership in this church. All such candidates shall be presented to the church at any regular church service for membership in any of the following ways:

1. by profession of faith and for baptism according to the policies of this church;

2. by promise of a letter of recommendation from another Christ-centered church, having been baptized by immersion;

3. by restoration upon a statement of prior conversion experience and baptism by immersion when no letter is obtainable;

4. by restoration upon request and their statement of faith; and

5. by Watch Care membership not to exceed six (6) months. Extension of Watch Care Membership may be granted upon recommendations of the Deacons to the Pastor.

SECTION 3. New Member Orientation

New members of this church are expected to immediately participate in the church's new member orientation class.

SECTION 4. Voting Rights of Members

Every member of this church thirteen (13) years of age and older, and in good standing, is entitled to vote at all elections and on all questions submitted to the church in conference, provided the member is present or provision has been made for absentee balloting. However, only members twenty-one (21) years of age and above shall be eligible to vote on matters such as buying, selling, or mortgaging of property, and obtaining financial loans. Good standing is defined as faithful attendance, financial support, and communication with the church.

Absentee ballot will be allowed only when considering the call or recall of the Pastor.

SECTION 5. Termination of Membership
Membership shall be terminated in the following ways:
1. death of the member;
2. transfer to another church;
3. exclusion by actions of this church which may be disciplinary; or erasure due to failure to maintain membership in good standing as defined in Section 4 above; and
4. erasure upon request or proof of membership in another church.

SECTION 6. Discipline
It shall be the practice of this church to emphasize to its members that every reasonable measure will be taken to assist any troubled member. The Pastor, ministerial staff, and Deacons are available for counsel and guidance. The attitude of members toward a troubled member shall always be guided by a concern for redemption rather than punishment.

If a serious condition exists which would cause a member to become a liability to the general welfare of the church, the Pastor and Deacons will take every reasonable measure to resolve the problem in accordance with Matthew 18. If it becomes necessary for the church to take action to exclude a member, a two-thirds (2/3) vote of the members present at a special call church meeting with a quorum present, as defined in Part V, Section 2 (Business Meetings) G, is required. The church will declare the person to be no longer in the membership of the church. All church proceedings shall be diffused by a spirit of Christian kindness and forbearance.

The church may restore to membership any person previously excluded, upon request of the excluded person, and by vote of the church upon evidence of the excluded person's repentance and reformation.

II. CHURCH ORDINANCES

SECTION 1. Baptism

The Pastor or his designee shall immerse those professing faith in Christ in the water. Immersion, as a believer, shall be a prerequisite to church membership.

SECTION 2. The Lord's Supper

The Lord's Supper shall normally be served to the assembled church by the Pastor, or his designee on the first Sunday morning of each month, or at such other time as may be decided by the Pastor and Deacons. Since it is the Lord's Table, none that are His shall be barred, but the Pastor shall frequently state the scriptural order, which places baptism as a prerequisite to the Lord's Supper, and shall explain the meaning of the Ordinances.

III. OFFICERS AND COUNCIL

All who serve as officers of the church and those who serve on church committees shall be members in good standing of this church, defined in Part I, Section 4 of the Bylaws.

SECTION 1. Church Officers

A. The officers of this church shall be the Pastor, the Deacons, and the Church Clerk, Assistant Clerk, Treasurer, Assistant Treasurer, Trustees, Budget Manager, Financial Secretary, Assistant Financial Secretary, Director of Christian Education, and the Superintendent of Sunday School.

B. No one shall be elected to office who has not been a member of this church for at least six (6) months, except that upon recommendation of the Pastor and the Deacons, a person may be considered by the church for office as deemed necessary, i.e. unfilled term due to death, illness, or transfer of membership. The Pastor will appoint/review after a one-year term the following positions: Chair and Co-Chair of Deacons, Deaconesses, Trustees, Missions, the Director of Christian Education, the Superintendent of Sunday School, Budget Manager, and Assistant to the Pastor.

C. All officers shall be twenty-one (21) years of age, spiritually mature, of unquestionable Christian character, loyal to the Word of God, dedicated and devoted to the Lord Jesus Christ and to the spiritual and material welfare of this church. They shall also be faithful in attendance and participation, both in regular services and business meetings of the church.

D. All elected officers shall assume their duties on the first day of January immediately following their election, to be held biannually on the last Sunday in October.

E. Retiring officers shall hold office until the term of the newly elected officers begin.

F. Any officer unable or unwilling to fulfill the duties of his office shall resign.

G. Upon the determination of an individual's inability to fulfill the duties of an elected office, that person, upon the recommendation of the Pastor and Deacons, and upon two-thirds (2/3) vote of the membership eligible to vote and present at a special call church meeting with a quorum present as defined in Part V, Section 2 G, shall be removed from office. This process may be eliminated if such person voluntarily submits his or her resignation in writing.

H. The term of office for all elected officers shall be two (2) years.

SECTION 2. The Pastor

A. Qualifications

1. A candidate for the pastorate shall be carefully examined by the pulpit committee as to his or her salvation, doctrine of Christian conduct, and call to the ministry. If the candidate has served in other churches, his or her ministry there should be explored. The candidate shall be required to state his or her acceptance of an adherence to the Articles of Faith, Constitution, and Covenant of this church. Any differences that the candidate holds concerning these documents should be submitted to the pulpit committee in writing. The candidate shall also state in writing any differences that he or she holds relating to groups and associations with which this church is in fellowship. The pulpit committee shall present only one person at a time for the consideration and vote of the church.

2. A candidate for the pastorate must be ordained and hold reputable credentials.

B. Election

When a vacancy of the office of Pastor occurs, the pulpit committee shall proceed, within thirty (30) days of its election, to find and recommend the name of a candidate to fill that office. Upon the recommendation of the pulpit committee and after the candidate has been heard by the congregation, action by the church shall be taken after notice has been given from the pulpit on two Sundays preceding the date of election. Approval by three fourths (3/4) of the qualified voting members present at a special call church meeting with a quorum present as defined in Part V, Section 2 G, shall be necessary for acceptance. Voting shall be by ballot.

C. Change of Pastor

1. The Pastor shall continue in office until he or she resigns or is dismissed by a three-fourths (3/4) majority of those present and qualified to vote at a special call church meeting with a quorum present as defined in Part V, Section 2 G, called for that purpose.

2. The Pastor may sever the pastoral relationship by written resignation, presented to the church for its action, provided that thirty (30) days notice of the decision to do so has been given. Should, at any time, the Pastor's beliefs or teachings fall out of accordance with the doctrinal standards of this church as given in the Covenant and the Articles of Faith, the Pastor's services shall be terminated by action initiated by the Ministry of Deacons and confirmed by the church. The church may sever the pastoral relationship when three fourths (3/4) of the qualified members join in written request to the Ministry of Deacons for change of Pastor. It shall then be the duty of the Chairman of the Ministry of Deacons to call a meeting of the membership to consider such change. Sixty (60) days previous notice of such a meeting shall be given by mail to each member and the Pastor. If, at said meeting, where a quorum is present and three-fourths (3/4) majority of the qualified voting memberships present and voting by ballot, there is a vote for change of Pastor, it shall be the duty of the clerk to so notify the Pastor and request his or her resignation to become effective immediately. Failure of the Pastor to comply with the request shall constitute sufficient grounds for the Ministry of Deacons to declare the office vacant.

D. Duties of the Pastor

It shall be the duty of the Pastor (1) to have charge of the spiritual welfare of the church; (2) to proclaim the gospel and lead church members in the proclamation of the gospel in the church and community; (3) to preside over services of public worship providing the leadership for such services, and to administer the church ordinances, namely the Lord's Supper and Baptism; (4) to conduct wedding ceremonies, funeral services, and infant dedication rites; (5) to provide Christian counseling and advice as required; (6) to care for the spiritual and physical being of the members and community, and to lead others in caring for fellow members as well as the community; (7) to lead the church in social action involvement; (8) to provide administrative leadership to effectively guide the church in the attainment of its mission; (9) to work closely with the Deacons in their training and performance in their work of proclamation of the Gospel and the building of the church membership; (10) to supervise the church staff members as is appropriate and provide for staff training and development; (11) to serve as an ex officio member of all ministries and committees. The Pastor shall act as moderator of church business meetings except when the relations between Pastor and church are presented for discussion.

SECTION 3. The Deacons
A. Qualifications
1. The scriptural qualifications for Deacons are found in 1 Timothy 3:8-13. Acts 6:1-8, as believed by many, discusses the appointment of the first Deacons and contains or lists additional information about the qualifications for that office. The Epistle of Paul to Titus contains further qualifications for the Deacons.
2. Deacons should be persons of wisdom, inspired by the Holy Ghost. They should be leaders, proven in their Christian character in the home, church, and community.

B. Appointment
1. Upon appointment as a "Deacon-in-Training" by the Pastor, the candidate will serve until successful completion of the Deacon Training Program, at which time, upon the recommendation of the Pastor and the Ministry of Deacons, the candidate will be appointed to the Ministry of Deacons.
2. An ordained Deacon uniting with this church must be a member for a period of not less than six (6) months, during which time he may, at the recommendation of the Pastor, serve as an Associate Deacon while completing the prescribed Deacon Training Program.

C. Number of Deacons
The number of Deacons shall not be less than seven (7). Appointments shall be made by the Pastor upon recommendation of the

Deacons to fill vacancies and to add to the number of Deacons as the church warrants.

D. Organization
1. The Body of Deacons will be known as the Deacons Ministry.
2. The Chairman of the Deacons Ministry will serve as a member of the Church Council.
3. Regular meetings shall be held monthly on a date set by the Deacons Ministry. Special meetings may be held at any time upon the call of the Chairman or Pastor. A majority of the ministry will constitute a quorum.

E. Duties
1. to proclaim the Gospel by personal witnessing, teaching, community evangelism, and to support and promote revival;
2. to care for the church members and other persons in the community; i.e., serving communion, visiting the sick and shut in;
3. to provide guidance and counseling as required and directed by the Pastor;
4. to assist in the development and administration of the mission outreach program and activities;
5. to serve as a council of advice with the Pastor in all matters pertaining to the welfare, administration, and mission of the church;
6. to work with the Trustees in the administration of church business matters;
7. to assist in the orientation and instruction of new members;
8. to assist the Pastor in the ordinances of Baptism and the Lord's Supper;
9. to be of moral support to the Pastor, accompany him or her (whenever and wherever possible) on outside preaching engagements;
10. to accompany the Pastor on home or hospital visitations or to make such visitations as needed or requested.

SECTION 4. The Deaconesses
The Deaconess Ministry is composed of women who, from their own Christian testimony, acceptance by the church, personal spiritual zeal, scriptural knowledge, and good work in missions and stewardship, become eligible for service in the Diaconate. Deaconesses are appointed by the Pastor (1 Timothy 3:8-13, Romans 16:1).

A. Qualifications
The deaconesses are wives of deacons and are also other dedicated
Christian women. The qualifications for the deacons set forth in
1 Timothy 3:8-13 hold true for the deaconess as well as the deacon.
Deaconesses are expected to possess the following qualifications:
1. high ideals, morals, and principles;
2. humility before the Lord;
3. even-temperedness in all things;
4. settled in religious faith;
5. a positive example in the home, community, etc.;
6. an inspiration to fellow church members;
7. able and willing to give up time to carry out the duties of the ministry;
8. loyal, dependable, and committed to service;
9. a support to the Pastor and the church.

B. Duties
1. assist the pastor, ministers, and deacons with various duties of the
church;
2. prepare the elements and set up the communion table for each
Communion Service;
3. ensure the pulpit cloths and communion linens are clean and in
good condition;
4. assist in the fellowship of new members;
5. assist the female candidates in preparation of and during baptism;
6. visit the sick and shut-in, send cards, fruit baskets, and prepare
meals as needed for the sick local body;
7. work diligently for the up building of the kingdom of God and support the ministries of this local body;
8. send letters to visitors; and
9. chairperson serves on the Church Council.

SECTION 5. Trustees
Trustees should have knowledge of the Bible as it pertains to the mission of the church. Other qualities desired in a Trustee are spiritual
sensitivity and vision, teamwork capabilities, flexibility, and some
skills in property and financial matters.
A. Qualifications
1. Candidate shall have been a member in good-standing for a period
of six (6) months prior to consideration for this office;

2. Candidate shall be under consideration for at least six (6) months prior to election to office;

3. The minimum age of Trustees shall be the minimum legal age twenty-one (21) required by the state of _____ (name of state). All Trustees shall be bonded.

B. Appointment

The Pastor shall appoint all Trustees to the Trustee Ministry and designate its chairperson.

C. Organization

1. The number of Trustees shall not be less than seven (7) and appointment shall be made to fill vacancies and to add to the number of Trustees as the church warrants;

2. The body of Trustees shall be known as the Trustee Ministry; and

3. Trustees shall serve a term of three (3) years, and shall be eligible for reappointment by the Pastor.

D. Duties

1. The Trustees shall have no power to buy, sell, mortgage, lease, or transfer property without a specific vote of the church, authorizing each action. When the signature of Trustees are required, they shall sign legal documents involving the sale, mortgage, purchase, or rental of property, or other legal documents related to church approved matters. They shall open bank accounts as needed.

2. The Trustees shall be responsible for the administration of church finances and purchasing including: counting and depositing of church monies; record keeping and reporting; disbursement of church monies as directed by church policy; procurement and related functions; administration of the church budget; and the establishment of salaries and benefits. They may be assisted in these functions by the Treasurer, Assistant Treasurer(s), Budget Manager, Financial Secretary, Assistant Financial Secretary(s), and Deacons.

3. The Trustees shall receive, hold in trust, and manage the use of church facilities and all property, bond, mortgages, investments, legacies, and gifts. They shall keep all church property in good repair and maintain adequate insurance.

4. Trustees shall maintain adequate security systems on all church properties and arrange for adequate insurance protection on church property and employees.

SECTION 6. The Church Clerk and Assistant Church Clerk
A. Qualifications
1. Candidates shall be members of this Church, in good standing, for six (6) months prior to election to office;
2. Candidates shall possess the following skills:
    a. meticulous and accurate record keeping;
    b. general working knowledge of office machines, procedures, and management;
    c. good writing, spelling, and speaking skills;
    d. accurate typing skills of at least 45 words per minute;
    e. good organizational skills;
    f. ability to compose and prepare letters and documents independently; and
    g. computer literacy.

B. Election
Candidates for these offices shall be nominated by the church body at the biannual nominating meeting.

C. Duties
1. maintain official church membership records, including up-to-date listing of membership for distribution to members only;
2. record baptisms, infant dedications, deaths, weddings, etc.;
3. prepare all required reports based on membership records;
4. ensure safekeeping and handling of official and legal documents;
5. prepare bulletins/programs for Sunday Worship services and other special observances;
6. coordinate preparation of programs for services or events sponsored by church auxiliaries;
7. prepare announcements and notices to be published in Sunday bulletins and in monthly newsletter;
8. keep up-to-date records of the sick and shut-in;
9. assist with the reception of new members;
10. perform general stenographic and clerical duties as required;
11. assist Office Manager with the management of the church office;
12. prepare baptismal and new member certificates;
13. write and/or update church history and prepare history for annu-

al publication;

14. administer the safe deposit box of the church;

15. keep a record of all business meetings of the church and the church council, entering the minutes of the meeting of the two groups in separate books;

16. perform other duties as assigned by the Pastor; and

17. the Assistant Church Clerk will serve as an assistant to the Church Clerk in all of the above duties and will assume these duties in his or her absence.

SECTION 7. The Financial and Assistant Financial Secretary

A. Qualifications

1. Candidates for these offices shall be members of this church, for six (6) months prior to election to office.

2. Candidates for these offices shall possess the following skills:

    a. meticulous and accurate record keeping;

    b. aptitude for figures;

    c. good organizational skills; and

    d. computer literacy.

B. Duties

The Assistant Financial Secretary will assist the Financial Secretary and shall assume the duties of the Financial Secretary in his or her absence. The Financial Secretary will, along with the Treasurer, maintain accurately the financial records and reports for the church; prepare and make quarterly and annual reports; maintain individual members' records and on a regular basis as designated provide to each member a record of contributions.

The Financial Secretary will prepare monthly financial reports; provide copies to any member upon request; assist in the preparation of the annual budget; and shall perform such other duties in connection with the administration of church finances as required or as the Church Advisory Council may designate.

C. Election
Candidates for this office shall be nominated by the church body at the biannual nominating meeting.

SECTION 8. The Treasurer and Assistant Treasurer
A. Qualifications
1. Candidates for these offices shall be members for at least six (6) months prior to election to office.
2. Candidates for these offices shall possess the following skills:
    a. meticulous and accurate record keeping;
    b. aptitude for figures;
    c. good organization skills;
    d. general knowledge of banking procedures;
    e. eligibility for bonding; and
    f. computer literacy.

B. Election
Candidates for these offices shall be nominated by the church body at the biannual nominating meeting.

C. Duties
The Treasurer will assist in the preparation of the annual budget and shall perform any other duties related to the administration of church finances as directed by the Church Council or Trustees. The Treasurer and Assistant Treasurer shall be bonded.

The Assistant Treasurer will assist the Treasurer, and will assume all duties of the Treasurer in his or her absence. The Treasurer shall maintain accurate records of all receipts and disbursements; write, sign, record, and mail all checks; prepare the monthly financial report and see that the Financial Secretary has what is required for updating membership records.

SECTION 9. The Superintendent of Sunday School and the Assistant Superintendent
A. Qualifications
1. Candidates for these offices shall have been members of the church in good standing for six (6) months prior to appointment.
2. Candidates for these offices shall possess good organization skills

and shall be Spirit-filled and have a working knowledge of the Christian Education Program.

B. Election
The Pastor shall appoint candidates for these offices.

C. Duties
The Superintendent shall have general supervision over the Sunday School. He or she is responsible for publicizing general Sunday School activities, staff recruitment, and will hold regular planning and training sessions. The Superintendent will select literature and materials with approval by the Pastor. The Assistant Superintendent will serve as directed by the Superintendent and in the absence of the Superintendent.

The Superintendent will serve as a member of the Church Council and will prepare a report to be presented at the scheduled council meetings and general church conferences.

SECTION 10. The Church Advisory Council
The Church Advisory Council shall set in place overall policies for the Church. The Church Advisory Council shall consist of all officers named in Article III Section I-A (except Assistant Officers) and two members-at-large elected by the Church body at its regular time of election of officers.

The Church Advisory Council shall meet quarterly for regular meetings. It shall meet for special meetings at the call of the Pastor, or in the absence of the Pastor, the Chairman of the Deacons Ministry.

The Clerk shall keep the minutes and include a report on the activities of this Council in his or her regular reports to the Church.

It shall be the duty of this Council to consider major matters of church business brought before it and present its recommendations to the church body for action.

The Council shall be chaired by the Pastor, and the Chairman of the Deacons Ministry in the Pastor's absence.

IV. CHURCH COMMITTEES
SECTION I. General
Committees shall be established and dissolved as deemed necessary unless otherwise indicated below.

SECTION 2. Budget and Finance Committee
The Budget and Finance committee shall consist of the Budget Manager, Financial Secretary, Treasurer, and three (3) designated Trustees. The Budget Manager shall serve as Chairperson.

The duties of this committee shall be to prepare the budget for the ensuing fiscal year for presentation to the church for its approval at a meeting called for that purpose approximately thirty (30) days prior to the beginning of each fiscal year.

The committee shall function throughout the year to recommend budget revisions to the church as may be deemed necessary.

At-large members of this committee shall serve for a period of two years.

The Pastor shall appoint the Budget Manager. The Chairperson of the Trustee Ministry shall appoint its (3) designees.

V. MEETINGS
SECTION 1. Public Worship
A. Public worship services shall be held regularly, morning and evening, as appropriate on the Lord's Day. These services shall not normally be given over to anything but prayer and the preaching and teaching of the Word, with an appropriate musical ministry. Any other special presentation shall be subject to approval by the Pastor and Deacons.
B. At least once each week there shall be Bible Study for prayer and praise.
C. It shall be the practice of this church to observe the Lord's Supper at least once a month, at which time the Covenant is read.

SECTION 2. Business Meetings

A. The official church year shall begin the first day of January and close the last day of December.

B. A nominating committee consisting of the Deacons Ministry shall prepare a slate of candidates to be presented to the Church for election of Church Officers.

C. The annual meeting to elect new officers shall be held no later than October 31.

D. The Church Conference shall be held in January and July of each year. All Officers and Heads of Ministries are responsible for preparation and presentation of reports at the Annual Church Conference.

E. Special business meetings may be called at any time at the discretion of the Pastor and/or the Deacons Ministry. Subject matter must be defined and only such matters will be transacted in such meeting.

F. Only members thirteen (13) years of age and above shall be eligible to vote. However only members twenty-one (21) years of age and above shall be eligible to vote on corporate matters such as buying, selling, or mortgaging of property, and obtaining financial loans.

G. Forty (40) members shall constitute a quorum.

SECTION 3. Order of Business Meetings

Suggested order of business:

1. Reading and approval of minutes of previous meeting
2. Clerk's report
3. Treasurer's report
4. Deacon's report
5. Trustee's report
6. Sunday School Superintendent's report
7. Church Council's report
8. Reports from other standing committees
9. Reports from departments of the church
10. Election of officers
11. Unfinished business
12. New business
13. Adjournment

VI. CHURCH ORGANIZATIONS

A. No organization of the church shall engage in any practice or hold any policy contrary to the general position of the church itself. All officers must hold membership in this church.

B. All organizations are subject to the control of the church in accordance with its constitution and approved church policies.

VII. MISSIONS

It shall be the policy of this church to support only missions engaged principally in evangelism and the establishment of Baptist churches (schools, hospitals, and similar ministries must be kept subordinate to the primary objectives). They shall be in agreement with our confession of faith, both in doctrine and practice. They shall be Baptist in both name and practice. Christian schools and social agencies, such as homes for the aged, children's homes, etc., shall be considered an appropriate part of the missionary program.

VIII. GENERAL

SECTION 1. Use of Church Property and Name

A. The Trustees shall approve use of the property for other than regularly scheduled meetings.

B. All gatherings off church property held in the name of the church shall be subject to the approval of the Pastor and Deacons. According to this constitution, this is to be handled in a separate meeting.

C. Fraternity and sorority organizations will be permitted to hold service upon approval of the Pastor and the Deacons Ministry.

D. Any visiting Pastor speaker must have the approval of the Pastor and Deacons.

SECTION 2. Pastor's Vacation and Salary

A. The Pastor shall have not less than two (2) weeks paid vacation each year.

B. The Pastor's salary shall be reviewed and determined at least once a year, with consideration given to rising costs of living.

SECTION 3. Monetary Principles

A. The systematic giving of money for the support and work of the Lord is worship as well as duty. It must be kept on the plane of voluntary free-will offerings, untarnished by any hope of material gain. All members are expected to give regular financial support to the church and to the advancement of the projects it shall sponsor. In determining the Lord's portion, we believe and affirm with the

Scriptures that at least one-tenth (1/10) of one's income should be faithfully and cheerfully given by each one (2 Corinthians 9:6-7). In addition each person, after giving the tithe, should give an offering.

B. A statement of each donor's account shall be given to him or her at the end of each year by the Financial Secretary. Numbered envelopes shall be provided to enable proper recordkeeping.

C. All church financial records shall be audited annually by an outside auditor.

SECTION 4. Legal Provisions

A. This church shall have the right to own, buy, or sell tangible properties, both real and personal, in its own name and through properly elected officers, when authorized by vote of the church.

B. No profit shall ever accrue to the benefit of any individual from the assets, holdings, or other transactions of this church. Contributions may be made only to other nonprofit organizations.

C. In the event of the dissolution of this corporation, all of its debts shall be fully satisfied. None of its assets or holdings shall be divided among the members or other individuals, but shall be irrevocably designated by corporate vote prior to dissolution to such other nonprofit religious corporations as are in agreement with the letter and spirit of the Articles of Faith adopted by this church, and in conformity with the requirements of the United States Internal Revenue Code of 1954 (Section 501 C-3).

IX. AMENDMENTS AND BYLAWS

A. This constitution may be amended at any annual church conference where a quorum is present and a three-fourths (3/4) majority of the qualified voting membership is present and voting by ballot.

B. The church may adopt from time to time such Bylaws in amplification hereof as may be necessary or desirable, and shall provide therein for amendment of the same.

C. This Constitution shall be reviewed every three (3) years.

Strategic Plan Checklist

Assessing the Church
• Determine the ministries, qualities, or activities for which your church is best known.
• Make a complete list of all your church's strong points. If possible, list them in general order of priority.
• Make a list of your church's weaknesses, the things your church does not do well. Again, list them in general order of priority.
• Survey the members of your church to determine their interests, skills, and talents. These are sometimes suggested by individuals' vocations and hobbies.
• Determine members' willingness to serve the church in some way.
• Assess the skill sets of individuals in the congregation.

Assessing the Community
• Describe the demographic makeup of your community—average and median age, income, occupation, church attendance, and any other particulars that might assist in your ministry.
• Make a list of the needs and interests that exist among the people in your community, and then prioritize them.
• Survey the land in your community; determine who owns it and how much of it is controlled by the city.
• Visit neighborhood churches to see what they do well and to determine their strengths and weaknesses.

Forming a Plan

• Determine possible "points of contact" between the church and the community.

• Explore how your church's strengths (as well as the talents and interests of church members) match up with the needs and interests you have listed.

• Determine which ministry activities constitute the best match between your church's abilities and the community's needs and what the budget implications of each of these ministries are likely to be.

• Determine whether any existing ministry within the church can take responsibility or if new ministries ought to be formed.

• Make a list of goals to set for your church to achieve in one year, three years, and five years from now. Define these goals in terms of creating new ministries, expanding existing ministries, adding disciples, and increasing the church's financial resources.

• Determine how each of these goals will be funded and how they will be pursued and achieved, including which persons and organizations within the church will be responsible for addressing them.

• Produce a concise, written document that expresses each of the church's goals for the next year, three years, and five years; how these goals will be funded; and who will be responsible.

Using the Plan as a Guide

• Get a copy of the strategic plan into as many hands as possible, especially those who are playing a role in carrying it out.

• Meet with small focus groups to get their "buy-in."

• Meet quarterly (or monthly if necessary) to assess the progress being made toward each goal and to make adjustments if necessary. Adjustments might include modifying the goal or recruiting new people in support of the goal.

Excerpts from the Greater Allen Employee Manual

THIS MANUAL HAS BEEN PREPARED TO INFORM YOU ABOUT THE ALLEN Church's employment practices, policies, and procedures, as well as the benefits provided to you as a valued employee and the conduct expected from you.

No employee manual can answer every question, nor would we want to restrict the normal question and answer interchange among us. It is in our person-to-person conversations that we can better know each other, express our views, and work together in a harmonious relationship.

We hope this Manual will help you feel comfortable with us. We depend on you—your success is our success. Please don't hesitate to ask questions. Your supervisor will gladly answer them. We believe you will enjoy your work and your fellow employees here. We also believe you will find Allen A.M.E. Church a good place to work.

We ask that you read this Manual carefully, and refer to it whenever questions arise. We also suggest that you share the information with your family so they can become familiar with our policies.

The Allen Church's policies, benefits, and procedures, as explained in this Manual, may be changed from time to time as church business, employment legislation, and economic conditions dictate. If and when provisions change, you will be given replacement pages for those that have become outdated.

What You Can Expect from Allen A.M.E. Church

Allen A.M.E. Church's established employee relations policy is to:

1. Select people on the basis of skill, training, ability, attitude, and character without discrimination with regard to age, sex, color, race, creed, national origin, marital status, or physical or mental handicap unrelated in nature and extent so as to reasonably preclude the performance of the employee.

2. Review wages, employee benefits, and working conditions constantly with the objective of providing maximum benefits in these areas, consistent with sound business practices compatible with similar churches in size as Allen A.M.E. Church.

3. Provide paid vacations and holidays to all eligible employees.

4. Provide eligible employees with medical and other benefits.

5. Develop competent people who understand and meet the objectives of the church, and who accept with open minds the ideas, suggestions, and constructive critiques of supervisors and fellow employees.

6. Make prompt and fair adjustment of any complaints that may arise in the everyday conduct of our business, to the extent that is practicable.

7. Respect individual rights, and treat all employees with courtesy and consideration.

8. Maintain mutual respect in our working relationship.

9. Provide buildings and offices that are attractive, comfortable, orderly, and safe.

10. Promote employees on the basis of their ability and merit related to available positions.

11. Make promotions or fill vacancies from within Allen A.M.E. Church whenever possible and warranted.

12. Do all these things in a spirit of Christian attitude and cooperation.

What Allen A.M.E. Church Expects from You
Your first responsibility is to know your own duties and how to do them promptly, correctly, and pleasantly. Secondly, you are expected to cooperate with management and your fellow employees and maintain a good team attitude. How you interact with fellow employees and those whom Allen A.M.E. Church serves, and how you accept direction, can affect the success of your work. In turn, the performance of one employee can impact the entire service offered by the Allen Church. Consequently, whatever your position, you have an important assignment: perform every task to the very best of your ability. The result will be better performance for the church overall, and personal satisfaction for you.

You are encouraged to grasp opportunities for personal development that are offered to you. This Manual offers insight on how you can positively perform to the best of your ability to meet Allen A.M.E. Church's employment expectations.

We strongly believe you should have the right to make your own choices in matters that concern and control your life. However, your lifestyle should be consistent with the tenants of Allen A.M.E. Church. We believe in direct access to management. We are dedicated to making Allen A.M.E. Church a place where you can approach your supervisor, or any member of leadership, to discuss any problem or question. We expect you to voice your opinions and contribute your suggestions to improve the quality of work at Allen A.M.E. Church.

The Allen Church's continued growth depends on the financial support of its members and visitors. As a member of the Allen A.M.E. Church family you share in the prosperity of Allen A.M.E. Church. All Allen A.M.E. Church employees are requested to prayerfully consider one's faithfulness to God through tithing of service and financial resources.

Remember, you help create the healthful, pleasant, and safe working conditions that Allen A.M.E. Church intends for you. Your responsibility, dependability, and integrity are vital as a staff member at Allen A.M.E. Church in making each working day enjoyable and rewarding!

Sample Event Budget

Club Name _____

Club Number _____ Date of Event _____

Description of Event _____

_____

Event Location _____

ESTIMATED TICKET SALE	Attendance	x Price	Estimated Revenue
Number of Adults			
Number of Children			
Number of Senior Citizens			
Free Will Offering			
	Estimated	Actual	Difference
Total Revenue			
Cost of the Event			
Artist/Musicians			
Sound System			
Printing			
Flowers & Presentations			
Bus Rentals			
Travel Expense			
Suppliers/gift bags			
Caterers			
Space Rental			
Hotels			
Other (specify)/cleaning			
Concessions			
Computer programmer			
TOTAL COST OF EVENT			
NET REVENUE			
NET REVENUE per person			

Club President _____ Date _____
Club Treasurer _____ Date _____

Approved By _____ Date _____
Approved By _____ Date _____

APPENDIX F

Sample Church Budget

CATEGORY	GENERAL LEDGER #	AMOUNT
CONTRIBUTIONS		
WEEKLY ENVELOPES	40100	327,954
RETURN CHECKS—		
WEEKLY OFFERINGS	40101	(2,830)
SHEKINAH LOOSE	40103	1,032
WEEKLY LOOSE	40105	5,668
MISSIONARY OFFERING	40110	5,551
SHEKINAH WEEKLY	40113	2,788
LOVE OFFERINGS	40115	952
SACRIFICIAL OFFERINGS	40118	2,384
SPECIAL WORSHIP	40125	6,460
WED. BIBLE STUDY	40128	963
CLUB INCOME	40135	(0)
SENIOR UTILITY		
REIMBURSEMENT	40220	59
DISCIPLESHIP MINISTRY	40235	76
DONATIONS: MEMORIAL FUNDS	40300	6
CLUB DONATIONS	40305	4,432
DONATIONS: OTHER	40310	1,018
MORTGAGE OFFERING	40311	148
Total CONTRIBUTIONS		356,661
OTHER INCOME		
ADMIN BOOKKEEPING SERVICES	40240	
MISC INCOME	40315	5,287
RENTAL INCOME	40320	853
COMMUNICATION		3,441
RENTAL INCOME	40330	
PAY PHONE	40400	12
REFUNDS	40430	13
EDUCATIONAL FUND	40550	316
MISCELLANEOUS INCOME	40600	377
GARNISH/DISCOUNT	49999	228
INTERFUND CLEARING	99999	29
Total OTHER INCOME		(12)
Total REVENUE		10,544
		367,205

CATEGORY	GENERAL LEDGER #	AMOUNT
EXPENSES		
Salaries & Employee Benefits		
PAYROLL REIMBURSEMENT FROM CLUB	50001	(3,454)
SALARIES	50100	102,987
FICA EXPENSE	50101	7,786
HEALTH INSURANCE	50103	7,937
LIFE INSURANCE	50104	694
NYS UNEMPLOYMENT INSURANCE	50105	1,527
WORKERS COMPENSATION	50106	920
DISABILITY INSURANCE	50107	128
ANNUITY	50108	507
FLEXIBLE DEPENDENT SPENDING	50109	168
PENSION/LIFE INSURANCE	50152	829
Total Salaries & Employee Benefits		120,029
Space Rental SCHOOL	50650	19,200
OTHER	50655	12
Total Rent		19,212
Parsonage & Pastoral		
HOUSING ALLOWANCE	50301	5,166
HOUSING ALLOWANCE	50302	3,792
HOUSING ALLOWANCE	50303	2,400
Total Parsonage & Pastoral		11,358
Printing & Office Supplies		
OFFICE EQUIPMENT	50520	39
AUDIO/VIDEO EQUIPMENT SUPPLIES & RENTALS	50521	3,241
LEASING EQUIPMENT	50522	1,567
POSTAGE/COPIER USAGE	50524	1,411
OFFICE SUPPLIES	50540	1,275
COMPUTER SOFTWARE & SUPPLIES	50542	3,723
POSTAGE	50546	559
PRINTING SERVICE	50830	2,121
JOURNAL ADS/ROCKS/PLAQ	50833	139
PHOTOGRAPHY	50836	44
DUES & SUBSCRIPTIONS/ MEMBERSHIP	50840	68
Total Printing & Office Supplies		14,187

CATEGORY	GENERAL LEDGER #	AMOUNT
Gifts, Honorarium & Donations		
DONATIONS & GIFTS	50580	2,225
DONATION - SCHOOL	50581	14,608
DONATIONS TO COLLEGES	50582	2,092
HONORARIUM	50585	4,891
EMPOWERMENT MINISTRY EXPENSE	50590	3,157
BENEVOLENCE	50805	250
Total Gifts, Honorarium & Donations		27,223
Professional & Consultants Fees		
SERVICE RENDERED-OTHER	50400	1,991
PROFESSIONAL FEES	50410	3,213
PROFESSIONAL FEES - LEGAL	50411	2,094
CONTRACTED COST	50415	2,323
CONSULTANT	50430	1,069
Total Professional & Consultants Fees		10,690
Telephone & Utilities		
TELEPHONE	50501	2,287
TUITION	50503	288
UTILITIES	50510	9,333
Total Telephone & Utilities		11,908
Travel, Travel & Meetings		
AUTO EXPENSE	50700	1,231
AUTO LEASING	50702	4,800
TRAVEL OUT OF TOWN	50710	2,409
TRAVEL TOLLS PARKING LOCAL	50711	401
CONFERENCE CONNECTED EXPENSE	50750	92
CONFERENCE ASSESSMENT	50752	8,934
Total Travel, Travel & Meetings		17,867
Repairs & Maintenance		
MAINTENANCE & REPAIR	50601	10,421
MAINTENANCE SUPPLIES	50602	8,397
GROUND MAINTENANCE	50605	1,158
EXTERMINATION	50610	184
Total Repairs & Maintenance		20,160
Insurance		
INSURANCE	50153	7,565
Total Insurance		7,565
Depreciation & Amortization		
DEPRECIATION EXPENSES	50925	12,060
Total Depreciation & Amortization		12,060

CATEGORY	GENERAL LEDGER #	AMOUNT
Interest Expense		
INTEREST EXPENSE	50920	551
Total Interest Expense		551
Other Expenses		
SECURITY	50455	441
CHURCH FURNISHINGS	50515	588
UNIFORMS/ATTIRE	50543	405
CHURCH SUPPLIES & FLOWERS	50544	3,545
PERMITS	50547	117
ROBES	50550	100
FOOD MINISTRY	50560	519
CATERERS	50561	1,302
OUTREACH MINISTRY	50564	191
MUSIC MINISTRY	50565	4,923
SENIOR CONGREG MEALS	50566	432
HOSPITALITY	50800	1,320
SCHOLARSHIP EXPENSES	50821	692
CABLE SERVICE	50832	905
PENALTIES	50842	225
WATER & SEWER CHARGES	50843	266
REAL ESTATE TAX	50844	341
PUBLIC MEDIA	50846	14,058
DISCIPLESHIP MINISTRY	50855	684
BANK CHARGES	50900	779
PAYROLL BANK CHARGES	50905	378
MISCELLANEOUS	60000	3,963
Total Other Expenses		36,174
Provision for Doubtful Receivable		
PROVISION FOR UNCOLLECTIBLES	80000	1,651
Total Provision for Doubtful Receivable		
Total EXPENSES		310,635
NET INCOME		56,570

Recommended Resources from Judson Press

Christian Education in the African American Church: A Guide for Teaching Truth by Lora-Ellen McKinney provides detailed practical guidance in virtually all areas of Christian education in the African American context.

Church Administration in the Black Perspective, Revised Edition by Floyd Massey Jr. and Samuel B. McKinney provides valuable insights on black church administration and includes technology updates and financial planning guidance.

The Church Business Meeting by R. Dale Merrill is a concise guide to parliamentary procedure in the church.

The Church in the Life of the Black Family by Wallace Charles Smith provides innovative ideas in education, employment, housing, and health care.

The Church Newsletter Handbook by Clayton A. Lord Jr. is a how-to guide for creating or improving church publications.

Church Officers at Work, Revised Edition by Glenn H. Asquith provides practical ideas for efficient church management.

Getting to Amen: 8 Strategies for Managing Conflict in the African American Church by Lora-Ellen McKinney offers ideas and insights to help churches manage conflict in general and as it relates to specific issues.

Our Help in Ages Past: The Black Church's Ministry Among the Elderly by Bobby Joe Saucer (with Jean Alicia Elster) issues a wake-up call to black church leadership everywhere to minister to and receive ministry from the black elderly.

Perfecting the Pastor's Art by G. Avery Lee and Gardner C. Taylor provides a rare opportunity to receive pastoral wisdom from two highly esteemed pastors, each of whom has been preaching for more than sixty years.

Rest in the Storm: Self-Care Strategies for Clergy and Other Caregivers by Kirk Byron Jones provides theological perspectives and practical advice focusing on the importance of self-care.

Total Praise! An Orientation to Black Baptist Belief and Worship by Lora-Ellen McKinney provides information on Baptist beliefs, perspectives on faith, and worship traditions in the African American context.

View from the Pew: What Preachers Can Learn from Church Members by Lora-Ellen McKinney provides African American preachers with in-sights from the pew to help them make sure they are sending the messages they want to send.

We Have This Ministry: The Heart of the Pastor's Vocation by Samuel D. Proctor and Gardner C. Taylor explores how to be a pastor who has integrity and character.

Work of the Church: Getting the Job Done in Boards and Committees by David R. Sawyer includes help for setting goals, adapting leadership styles, and building a team.

The Work of the Church Treasurer, Revised Edition by Thomas E. McLeod is a complete accounting manual with each procedure fully illustrated.

The Work of the Church Trustee by Orlando L. Tibbetts covers every facet of the trustee's responsibility.

The Work of the Clerk, New Edition by M. Ingrid Dvirnak shows how the work of the clerk is essential to the local church.

The Work of the Deacon and Deaconess by Harold Nichols covers the origin of the diaconate, qualifications, organization, ordinances, worship, the unchurched, training, and more.

The Work of the Pastor by Victor D. Lehman addresses core pastoral duties including conflict management, worship preparation, transitions, team ministry, identifying giftedness, and administration.

Work of the Pastoral Relations Committee by Emmett V. Johnson explains how to organize the committee, describes the functions, and outlines the benefits.

The Work of the Sunday School Superintendent by Idris W. Jones guides an inexperienced first-timer and gives new insight to the experienced.

The Work of the Usher by Alvin D. Johnson is a complete guide to the ministry of the usher, suitable for individual or group study.

The Work of the Worship Committee by Linda Bonn addresses such topics as how the worship service can reflect the mission and identity of the church.